DATE DUE

THE SEARCH FOR HELP:
A STUDY OF THE RETARDED CHILD
IN THE COMMUNITY

The Search for Help:

A Study of the Retarded Child in the Community

JERRY JACOBS, Ph.D.

BRUNNER/MAZEL, *Publishers* ● New York, N. Y.

Published by
BRUNNER/MAZEL, INC.
80 East 11th Street
New York, N.Y. 10003

Library of Congress Catalog Card No. 75-91923
SBN 87630-019-0

MANUFACTURED IN THE UNITED STATES OF AMERICA

Foreword

THE HISTORY of human anguish is as vast as it is interminable. That the anguish surrounding mental retardation is second to none would seldom be disputed by those who have experienced it—by parents, siblings, or the retarded persons themselves, or by those who have attempted to treat or to help such persons. Neither can there be any doubt that mental retardation is a social phenomenon—in every sense of the word—yet the social sciences have been strangely slow to bring their theoretical perspectives to the study of mental retardation. Anyone remotely familiar with the whimsical history of scientific fad and fancy should not be surprised by the reluctance of the social sciences to engage themselves in the search for an improved understanding or amelioration of mental retardation. Still, we can lament this general reluctance, just as we can applaud when we discover that a social scientist has turned his attention to the social phenomenon we have come to speak of as mental retardation.

Dr. Jacobs' report is doubly welcome, for it is not only a sign of a growing interest in the sociology of mental retardation, it is a book that renews and expands our acquaintance with the human realities of life in a society in which some among us become known as mental retardates. That these realities are presented in the words of the parents, siblings or teachers who have most intimately known the mentally retarded children, makes this book at once more dramatic and more illuminating.

The first portion of the book focuses upon parents' approaches to physicians in search of a hopeful diagnosis for their child. These encounters between troubled parents and their physicians are pure horror, as frustrating to one party as the other. As both parents and physicians misunderstand the others' part in these confused and painful exchanges, imputations of cowardice, in-

v

It is plain to see

competence, indifference, and psychological inadequacy abound. We see all too vividly—that the responsibility of labeling a child as a mental retardate is one which physicians may be poorly trained to perform. We also see the torment of parents as they attempt to evade the stigma of that awesomely unacceptable diagnosis—mental retardation.

In turning to the education of the retarded, we discover, as expected, the self-fulfilling character of the diagnosis of mental retardation. And, we again see inadequacy—this time in the preparation of the school system and its teachers for the task of educating the "uneducable." The work of Dexter, and others, has well prepared us to hear such doleful tales as these, but in the use of retarded children as *teachers* of other retarded children a most promising prospect is offered. Here, perhaps, is an answer to much that now impairs the self-esteem and the learning ability of many retarded children.

Finally, Dr. Jacobs returns to the parents of the retarded, and their feelings about the present and the future. From the work of such sociologists as Farber and Mercer we already know something about the effects of a retarded child upon his family. We know about the disruption, but we know, too, that positive feelings of the parents and siblings of the retarded children discussed in this study are remarkable; the strength and consistency of these feelings warrant careful consideration.

The families represented in this research are few, and we cannot be certain that their experiences or feelings are typical. For one thing, most of these families are Catholic; for another, the most common diagnosis of their retarded children is mongolism. Despite these cautionary notes, this research is a valuable addition to that thin shelf of books that represent the contributions of social science to the study of mental retardation. The book is a sobering report of human suffering, and of foolishness, but it is also a harbinger of hope.

ROBERT B. EDGERTON, PH.D.

The Neuropsychiatric Institute
University of California
Los Angeles, California

Preface

THE AUTHOR'S INITIAL involvement in the study of mental retardation began with his employment as a sociologist with a mental retardation training program for physicians. Early in this period, by way of an orientation to the subject, I took a number of field trips to various residential facilities, workshops, and schools for the retarded. I observed numerous doctor-patient interactions and talked informally and at length with both pre-school parents and teachers of the retarded in various school settings. Through these encounters and observations, it came to my attention that parents of retarded children had several key concerns regarding the well-being of their child and the rest of the family, and had initiated certain search procedures in an attempt to resolve them. These concerns fell into three basic categories: 1) a desire for a definitive, relatively favorable diagnosis and prognosis for their child; 2) an answer to the question of where the child would go upon leaving the pre-school; and 3) some resolution to the question of the child's fate from adolescence on, with particular emphasis on what would become of him after their death.

The parents' greatest effort with respect to the first concern (where they felt there was any real hope for success) had for many already taken place prior to the author's initial contact, i.e. within the first 5-6 years of the child's life. This is not to say that the parents had by this time abandoned hope; they had not. But their hope was based not so much upon the professionals' evaluation of the situation as upon their own faith. The above parental outlook rested at least in part upon certain ambiguities introduced by professionals in the course of evaluating their child's physical and intellectual status and potential.

The search for a resolution to the second concern was already under way. In this regard, the parents had initiated a grooming program for the child, in an attempt to maximize his chances for acceptance at the only public facility for "trainable" retarded children between the ages of 8 and 18 in San Francisco.

The search for an answer to the third question—the parents' demise and its consequences for the child—had been with the parents from an early date. It was not an issue the parents had often discussed with others, but when they did, they had received little help in their efforts to deal with it. Included in their future concerns was the parents' anxiety regarding the child's status as an adolescent. Would it be possible to manage him at home or would they have to institutionalize him after all and lose all that they—both parent and child—had worked so hard to accomplish?

These three concerns correspond roughly to three time periods—their past and present experiences and future expectations. All of these concerns and the interactions they occasioned will be dealt with in detail in the following chapters.

The information contained in this manuscript stems from three main sources. First, there are the tape-recorded interviews with fourteen mothers whose children were enrolled in a San Francisco pre-school for retarded children. These interviews averaged an hour and a half in length and were conducted by the author at the pre-school and at the convenience of the parents. Before the interviews took place, the author had been introduced to the parents and was on good terms with them, as a result of having spent an average of five hours a week over a six-month period observing both the children and the parents at the school. The parents' participation in the interviews was on a voluntary basis, and all but three parents who had children at the school during this period asked to be interviewed. The interviews were conducted in an informal manner and covered seventeen points, e.g. family expectations for the child, changes in parental attitudes over time toward the child, their extent of participation in outside groups, etc. All parents were asked the same set of questions but not necessarily in the same order. The tape recordings were subsequently transcribed and the data analyzed.

The second source of data were the case records of a large San Francisco mental health clinic offering therapy and evaluation services to retarded children and their families.

Finally, the data from transcribed tape-recorded interviews with ten teachers of retarded children in different institutional settings within a seventy mile radius of San Francisco was also incorporated. These averaged an hour and a half in length and covered, again in no set order, specific topics which all of the teachers were asked to comment on. All of these sources of data were then evaluated and integrated into what constitutes the main body of the author's work.

JERRY JACOBS

TABLE OF CONTENTS

THE SEARCH FOR HELP:
A STUDY OF THE RETARDED CHILD
IN THE COMMUNITY

CHAPTER I

Problems of Diagnosis and Prognosis: Parents, Practitioners and Outlooks

UPON FIRST LEARNING that their child was retarded, the parents in this study saw themselves faced with choosing one of three possible alternatives: 1) taking the child home, 2) having him institutionalized or 3) murdering him. The careers of these mentally retarded children had much in common. First, there was the discovery of the child's retardation, the initial shock, disbelief, and/or qualified acceptance, or a complete lack of appreciation or understanding of what the diagnosis meant. This period was followed by a desire to somehow be rid of the child, have him placed, or failing this, murder him. Having decided not to be rid of the child immediately, there was a cooling off period and a reassessment of the situation, so that the parent was willing to undertake a kind of trial run, always keeping in reserve the possibility of future placement if things didn't work out, i.e. if the child failed to improve, became unmanageable, or otherwise put the family in jeopardy. During this period, the parents often initiated a search for professional help in the form of a diagnosis and prognosis and/or assistance in the more concrete form of how to deal with the child's day to day problems. Many of these problems in the early stages were of a medical nature. This and the fact that most evaluation centers are situated in medical settings led the parents into a series of encounters with doctors.

The sequence of events presented above did not always occur in that order. There was much overlapping. Parents often held many contradictory feelings and beliefs simultaneously. For ex-

1

ample, it was not uncommon for parents to state that they were aware of their child's limitations and restricted future prospects, and in the same breath state that there is considerable disagreement among the experts and "you never can tell." A more specific example of the general case noted above is something like "you can't expect much from Johnny . . . you ought to see how smart he is." Most parents interviewed, no matter how "realistic" their appraisal of their child's condition, had no trouble in incorporating this contradiction. A partial explanation for this phenomenon is the ambiguity the parents encountered from the very start in the course of seeking professional help.

DOCTOR-PARENT INTERACTIONS

Parents of retarded children often received contradictory diagnoses and prognoses while "shopping" for an optimistic opinion. Information sometimes proved not only contradictory but false. Apart from the inexact state of the medical sciences and the resultant inconsistencies encountered from one expert to another, there was the problem of no information or misinformation that accrued to the parents seeking professional advice. I refer here to the difficult time the parents had in getting the professional to reveal his findings or, if he did reveal them, to explain them so as not to leave it to the parents to construct their meaning for themselves. This was often the case, and the results for the parents and child ranged from disruptive to disastrous. Ehlers has this to say about the professional handling of information transfer.

> "Time and again the mothers mentioned wanting to hear about their child in a sympathetic and compassionate manner. Apparently there is much that needs to be learned about how to talk to and with parents about their retarded children. . . . How the parents are told certainly seems quite as important as what they are told . . . there is a definite implication for the physicians in the mothers' reporting a need for an understanding and understandable manner of communicating the diagnosis and prognosis"[1]

Then, too, professionals tended to discount the accounts of the parents with respect to their assessment of the child's potential via their own direct observations. It need hardly be pointed out that the doctors' skepticism in accepting the parents' accounts did little to help establish the rapport considered so necessary for a successful therapeutic encounter. One parent put it this way:

"I think one of the things along these lines that has disturbed us most of all is that we went to see a doctor or something, explaining that Paul already does this (something the specialist said he would be incapable of doing) like crawl or sort out blocks or something like that, and having lived with him day and night for several years, ah, he doesn't do it in the doctor's office, you get sort of a stare, like you probably stacked the blocks for him or you probably sorted them out for him; you know, this sort of complete disbelief based on a half-hour's observation when the child was obviously disturbed being in a strange environment. And then sometimes after he's been in a nursery school or something and he starts doing this thing that he's already . . . we've seen him do a number of times, immediately the staff says, haven't we done marvels for this child, he's now doing this. You know, it's the complete and utter disbelief in our own observations that we find more irksome, particularly when we realize that when we've observed a child for a good portion of the day every day of the week and here's someone who has only seen him in a strange environment and the child isn't doing what he normally would do for a very brief period of time. That's one of the more irksome things I think we've experienced . . ."[2]

In light of the above, it is perhaps not surprising to find that:

"As far as the mothers were concerned, the public health nurse then was very strongly identified as *the* important service. . . . Another service, mentioned about as often as the public health nurse, was the nursery school. Again, granting that this is an important service, one wonders why mothers seem to have it uppermost in their thoughts. Why didn't they mention the psychologist or the physician more often? These latter two services are most important in providing data for proper evaluation of the child. Yet, unless probed for further information, as to 'what else helped,' the mothers most often mentioned only the nurse, the nursery school, and, further down the list, the speech therapist."[3]

Ehlers concludes that the administrators of clinical programs frequently ignore the perspective of those seeking help, as well as the effects of this oversight upon the programs' effectiveness.

". . . clinical directors may find some of the mothers' opinions regarding services helpful in future planning. These opinions may be faulty as viewed by the clinic, but they represent 'reality' to the mothers. Truth in this case may rest more on how the mothers view the services and her needs, and not so much on whether or not she is right in her judgment."[4]

The above findings are supported by those of Kramm and others. Two-thirds of the mothers of retarded children in her sample were "definitely dissatisfied" with the doctors' way of handling their orientation to the problem and felt that it had deepened the "shock of discovery" and prolonged their period of comeback.[5] The author's data also tend to support this. Perhaps the best way to appreciate the importance of the professional's acknowledging, respecting and trying to incorporate the parents' point of view is to see what happens when he fails to do so. The following are the transcribed verbatim accounts of five mothers of retarded children in the author's series, dealing with their professional encounters during their search for help.

Mother: Well of course we knew John was mongoloid shortly after he was born. Matter of fact it wasn't any more than twenty minutes after they brought me back to my room. And ah, the doctor told my husband in the hallway of his deficiency and they called the family doctor and he told them to call in the pediatrician. So they called in the pediatrician and they checked him over and they felt definitely that he was mongoloid. So it was—it wasn't really, I don't think any more than a half hour afterwards that we found out. And my obstetrician is one of these very sensitive-type people. Most doctors do not display their emotions on their face, but he

is one of the few. Now I should have—I should have sensed
something in the—in the delivery room—that something was
bothering him because he teased me about having another
boy. And John was, he wasn't grotesque looking, but he was
funny looking. He was tiny, but he was real pudgy looking.
I noticed how chubby his little hands were and I made
a comment about this. And I noticed how puffy his little
eyes were, but I didn't say anything about that. But the thing
that I thought was strange was that he was thrusting his
tongue. Which I thought—well, I don't know, maybe some
babies come out all kinds of ways when they're first born,
you know. Cause my oldest was one of these exceptionally
pretty babies. Well, you can't always have a pretty boy, you
know. And he, there was an intern in the room and there
were several student nurses and of course they're all saying
how cute and I kept saying, well he's not as cute as my first
one was, you know. The doctor still didn't say anything, you
know. And then when he had gone out and told my husband,
my husband came into my room and he already knew that
see—and I said to him, gee are you that disappointed because—no, well when I went out of the delivery room I told
him he was the father of a funny-looking little son, is what
I told him. I couldn't help it. He was funny looking. And
then after that the doctor told him. And then when he came
down to my room I said to him, I said, are you that disappointed because it wasn't a girl—cause he really wanted a
girl. No, no, no, he said. I said, well what's the matter with
you? What is it? And he said, nothing. And I said, well maybe this will be a quiet boy, because the other one was such
a loud mouth. And you know he was just acting so strangely
and by then you get all these apprehensive feelings which I
had during the pregnancy anyhow. And then the doctor came
in and he drew the curtains around my cubicle and I thought,
oh no, you know. And he told me the baby was born completely healthy, but he's not completely normal. And I looked
at him and I said, he's mongoloid. And I've never seen a
mongoloid baby before in my life, but all of a sudden the
flat features, the thrusting of the tongue, you know, just kind
of hit me in the face. And that poor doctor couldn't bring
himself to say the word. He said, it shouldn't have happened
to you, not to your age bracket. He said, but they're not,

sure yet. The pediatricians are going to check him and they're going to take tests and X-rays and so forth and so on. And then after this, the pediatrician did come down and said that they felt that he definitely was. He had enough of the characteristics, you know, that they felt that he was, but they were going to take X-rays of the pelvis and the skull. And ah— I still maintain that doctors only tell you what they want you to know. Because I snuck a look at the X-ray report one day in the pediatrician's office several months afterwards and the diagnosis was, well the skull—one side showed the mongoloid deformity and the other side didn't. And the navel zones were normal and the pelvis, one side was normal and one side was mongoloid degree, or whatever it is. And so the diagnosis was "possibly mongoloid," but they didn't tell me the worst possible, see. The poor pediatrician, I mean he didn't know us, he didn't know our personalities or our temperament. Naturally, he knew human emotions. But you know, temperaments react differently too. And I felt so sorry for him after I got over it because I just lay there and practically screamed at him that I just couldn't take that baby home and love him without pitying him. And if I pitied him, I would ruin him. And I just couldn't do it, you know. And he went on to tell us it was very costly to put him in a private home. You know, that it wasn't that easy to put him in an institution. And he said, ah—he was trying to get us to realize that it wasn't easy to do these things. But yet, I guess he kind of understood a little how we felt. And yet not knowing us, I don't think the poor guy really knew quite what to say. You know, and ah—of course he said, well, I can't tell you anything of how the baby is going to develop or anything. He says, because we just don't know. And he says, I realize that your husband would like black and white statistics, but I can't give them to him. We're just sitting on a fence. Well, I asked him if there was any literature or anything we could read, and he said, no that there was nothing, you know. And of course this was on a Thursday and that evening we were just like two zombies. We did nothing but cry. Bill went to the Catholic social service. He went to see anybody that he could think of to see where we could put this child. I think we would have dumped him into a garbage can if we'd had half a chance. And the next day we kind of felt the same way still. Bill was even a little bit more in his intenseness of the feeling—ah, than I was. A mother always I think has a feeling, well, she went through this pregnancy, she had the pain. The father has a different feeling about it. They don't go through the pain end of it. And you know, the pain gives you a closer tie. So—ah he still tried the next day and there was, you know, nothing we could do. And the obstetrician said, well why don't you maybe put him in a foster home for a week or two until you get home and you're feeling better. You'll look at things differently then. And late that afternoon, I guess it was around the dinner hour, some friends of mine came by to see me. And I was really at my worst. I even thought I could take this child home and smother it and they would attribute it to crib death. And I said, they're just not going to make me take that baby home. If it happened to them, they wouldn't want it either. You know, I just went through everything you could think of. And they went off, and for some strange reason I kind of dozed off and I saw this little boy sitting at my dinner table, and I knew it was John. And it was like God was tapping me on the shoulder and saying, Listen lady, listen to what those doctors are telling you. You don't know what the child is going to be like. You at least have to give him half a chance. And when I woke up, I just kind of had this funny feeling. I thought, this is my child. I just can't put him away, even if I only can take him home for two or three weeks. I at least have to try to do what I'm supposed to do."

A second mother gave this account:

Mother: Well, do you want to start from the time he was born?

Int.: Yeah. Right.

Mother: All right. He was born premature and at the age of three months he had meningitis. And as far as anyone knows, the meningitis is what has retarded him. It's not fact. It's just theory, that's what they think. They don't know that he wasn't born like this, but they said that meningitis left him with the cerebral palsy condition. So this is what we work on. And he has progressed very slow up until his 6 years and the nicest thing that ever happened was getting him to come out to the Pre-school, because up until then we just got kind of shuffled back and forth from one place to another. We had ordered a psychological evaluation on Eric and they told me that they had set up a date for it and had ordered it and so I took Eric out and had his evaluation and that was the last I heard of it except when I got the bill for $17.50. I never heard anything from it. Nothing. And that was my biggest complaint about the situation; every time you ask a question, you're answered with a question. There's no, there's no facts given. And I don't think it's really fair because when you go into this, it's new, it's never happened to you before, you don't know what to expect, you don't know which way to turn, or where to go. . . .

Int.: Was one of the things you were worrying about, thinking about then, how much Eric would develop and how far you could expect him to go and what to expect of him?

Mother: Right. We still don't know. We still don't know. We just go from day to day and I assume he will talk eventually because he does have speech. He does say "Ma Ma." He can say "No." His speech is there, but how much he will ever talk is another question too that there's no answer to. But we were also told he wouldn't walk and he walks now. So we just are patient now, and I'm sure he'll say something eventually; when, that's another thing. Of course that's something you can't do anything about. You just have to wait for it.

Int.: How did you and your husband feel when you first found out about the retardation and when he got meningitis and so on, those kinds of things?

Mother: Well, the meningitis was a very bad thing because we didn't know if he was going to live or not. There was two weeks there that I didn't know. At the end of two weeks my doctor told me that there was no doubt that Eric would survive. And the thing from then on was to prevent damage to his body, his facilities. So we just . . . he went from there on, my doctor went under the assumption that he was deaf, for the simple reason that in 90% of the cases of meningitis that he had been affiliated with, deafness was the handicap that was left. So he assumed that Eric's slowness was because he was deaf. And after Eric was about a year old, we kept insisting that he could hear. We kept insisting that he could hear, he could hear. And finally when he was two, the doctors really understood that Eric could hear. We got a radio out and turned it on and he knew then. So we went for hearing tests. Well of course when he had the hearing tests and the hearing tested out fine, then he told me maybe we weren't quite so lucky. Because it would have been easier if he had been deaf. Because when it wasn't the hearing, it was mental. . . .

Int.: How did that take you and your husband when you heard about it?

Mother: Well, you don't know what to think because you really don't know what's wrong with him. And you go into this just like you're blindfolded and nobody says anything. I . . . to this day I don't know whether they actually classify Eric as brain-damaged or mentally retarded, or what.

Int.: Did you try to call them or find out what . . .

Mother: Well, we had consultations and it just seems like it's one big series of questions, questions, questions, questions. And the doctor said that . . . the last time I spoke with her that . . . which was after the evaluation, that Eric would never walk, that he would probably walk with crutches, but that he wouldn't be able to walk and that we would have to be prepared to find permanent care for Eric. And she, at the time, did not elaborate on. . . .

Int.: . . . where or how or . . .

Mother: . . . or how much, or anything like that. And of course I have Eric with me most of the time. By the time you get through getting questioned, you're ready to go home. And there's nothing really definite, no. So we just go from one place to the next and from one day to the next. It's just such . . . nothing is down in black and white. I know he's had an EEG, but what that showed—there was never anything done. My own doctor finally told me that if they ever decided to do another one that it wouldn't show anything only that Eric had an abnormal brain pattern. But other than that, it wouldn't show anything. So it's just been more or less a matter of somebody throwing you in the water and' you just have to learn to swim, that's what it is. It's an awful, awful thing because it seems like you're just never going to find your way out of it, this maze that you're in.

The following are excerpts from a third parent taken from a tape-recorded interview:

Mother: It more or less started out like this: When Norman' was born, everything went normal and I had an old-fashioned doctor who didn't believe in telling the parents. When Norman was six months old he came down with bronchial pneumonia and almost died. And we rushed him into the hospital. And they told us he was mongoloid. And I couldn't accept it and neither did he. But ah, so then he was in there for about a week and I took him out and took him in to my own doctor which I had when I was pregnant with Norman and he told me at that time that he was mongoloid, which was six months later. So I was very upset and so was my husband and I didn't want any more kids and then I found out I was already pregnant two months with my last child. So that complicated matters all the more. For about six months, I myself think I lived in a nightmare is the way that I felt about it. . . . I think it's been the worst . . . when it came to almost losing him, and in April the doctor told us, it was just that close. And ah, at the time when it happened, I called my husband up and of course, just like he said and just like we had talked about later and like I mentioned a minute ago, with Norman you have to rush and when he's working he just can't drop everything and rush off to be with me, and so I went through that episode by myself. And it was rough. I sat up with him all night before he went into the hospital. Then I called the doctor throughout the night and he was telling me what to do and I kept telling him that nothing was helping, and he wouldn't believe me and we've been on the outs about that for quite a while now. My private physician for my children doesn't really even talk about Norman to me. In fact the first time I ever met this doctor I walked into his office and he says, you know, eventually you'll have to have this boy institutionalized. And I looked at him and I thought: yeah, from your viewpoint, but not from mine. Because I knew right then and there that my husband and I had gone through that experience once before and it was no fun. (The child had been institutionalized for a six-month period when he was one-and-a-half years old). I mean I'd rather keep him at home with me and pick up after him twenty-four hours a day than say: here son you're going over here and have him lose everything that it's taken him seven years to gain. And so at that time, I says, yeah, maybe. He's never brought it up again, and whenever I try to start a conversation about Norman, he's you know . . . I've got to do this and that — he just has no interest in talking about it.

Int.: Did you ever talk to any other doctors about it?

Mother: I talked to the doctor when we were going in for an evaluation.

Int.: Mmmmmm. What did they think there?

Mother: Well, he more or less feels that he hopes and thinks that Norman may talk some day because on the test that he had he was coming along pretty good, his IQ as I remember he said was approximately 4 which he didn't feel was very bad for Norman—it was about half of what it should be. And so that made me feel fairly good. One doctor felt that Norman may not be a mongoloid, that he may just have hyperthyroid, and my hopes went up zoom—straight up in the air, if you know what I mean. And then I started thinking and going back in my mind to all the doctors that I have spoken to, just briefly, and they all said, well he's mongoloid. And I mean for just one doctor to pop up out of the clear blue sky and say well, it might not be, I just couldn't believe it. And so I went back in to see my private physician and took Norman with me and I told him about it. And he says, Norman is mongoloid. He says he has no hyperthyroid condition at all. And I says, OK. So I mean, zoom, . . . right back down again. And, ah, so we just live with the fact that he's mongoloid. Now then my doctor did say something just last week when I took him to see about a cold that Norman's had. And I said, the life expandment on these retarded children is getting longer, isn't it. And he said, yes, it is. I mean you try to strike up something and he just answers you with a short comment and turns you right off. So I mean, I can't say: Sit down. We're going to talk about it. Because I mean I just haven't got that in me either. And I feel if he doesn't want to talk about it, I'm not going to force him. . . . But there's really nothing I want to know more about Norman, not at the immediate time. But it just kind of . . . I like to hear the doctor say himself how he feels Norman is coming along. You know, is there progress? Is it getting more worse? Do you think he may learn this? How far will he get with this? And stuff like that. That's what I would like him to tell me."

A fourth mother gave this account of her experiences with physicians in seeking help for her child:

Mother: When Heather was born the experience of giving birth to her was very good. I participated in a program called "Educated Childbirth" and I was awake, my husband was with me, took pictures. The doctor . . . finally the baby came and there was much joy. He held her up and he said, you have a beautiful baby girl. And he tried to put her thumb in her mouth. And she wouldn't suck it. And now looking back, that was the beginning. And when I tried to nurse her, no milk came in. And I was desperate, she wouldn't suck. I got myself in a real panic. The nurse came in and she held the baby and she held my breast and she tried to squeeze milk into that child and if you could squeeze out a drop onto her tongue, she would swallow. That was the beginning. I can't say that intellectually I thought my God —I know that lack of sucking, the extreme startled reflex, and this tiny stature and the heavy brows, the blunt nose, the underdeveloped chin, and the large low-set ears, I didn't know then. But I felt it. Something was wrong. I was having trouble.

Int.: When did you find out officially about it?

Mother: Well, I found out after months of this kind of thing day and night; the child not eating and begging my physician to do something, do something. Is there something wrong. And he didn't answer me. Then when she was 5 months old, he gave me phenobarbital to give her. And I was trying to give it to her and she fought against anything being put in her mouth. Which is a peculiar thing, the easiest thing to do is to eat, to drink. And she gasped when I put the spoon in her mouth and she began to choke and make peculiar sounds and I thought she was choking to death, and she'd inhaled the phenobarb and I knew it was very serious to have fluid in your lungs, you could drown on a teaspoon, a baby could. So I snatched her up and rushed her to the emergency room at the hospital. And they took one look at her and called upstairs for a pediatrician, a resident. A young Chinese woman doctor came down and she said, she asked me things that frightened me, that were more frightening than anybody telling me. She said what does the physician say about this edema. Edema! I thought she just had bad feet and bad hands. And I knew what edema was. Nothing, he hasn't said anything. And she mentioned the child's features and everything, her development; she couldn't shut her hand on anything. Anyway this young doctor said her lungs were clear, but she said a lot of other things by these questions, in just getting the history which she needed, she told me a lot. I went home and I called my doctor and I was crying. He'd never heard me cry before. I'd cried a lot, but never in front of him.

Int.: Was this a private physician?

Mother: Yes. Dr. G. I said that she said some awful things to me about the child's eyes, about the edema, about the features, about her development. And I said, up until now I've been saying, is there something wrong. Now, good God, I know there's something wrong. I've known it all along, why . . . you know, what is wrong—what is there. And he said, I will come by your house in the morning. Well, he had never done anything like that before. He said, I want to talk to you. And I'll see you at 7:30 before I start my rounds. Well, he couldn't have said . . . it was like the death sentence. I cried and cried and screamed all night long. Because his saying "I'll come" meant it's happening. Everything you feared is true. And he came and he said that she was not up to other babies her age, that he didn't want me to be alarmed but he thought I should take her—he was not an expert on this, or anything else for that matter—for an evaluation. And I was shocked at those words. But I agreed. I didn't resist at all. I didn't say: It can't be true. He's out of his mind. I knew it was true. So I took her very soon after to see the doctor and she took one look at her and said " 'Turner's Syndrome.' You do have a defective child." I was relieved. Because from that first day in the nursery I knew I had trouble. And all of that time I had accused myself, blamed myself, whipped myself. I was up all night and all day. I knew that a child who got what he needed would be contented, would be peaceful, would be happy. That is if I fed her right—I wasn't feeding her right. Do you know that I paid 50 cents a day for goat's milk? I had a special dairy bring me fresh goat's milk every morning. I rocked her in my arms until I ached all over, until I couldn't move. I carried her everywhere. I didn't use an infant seat. I didn't let her cry. I fed her on demand. And I thought what am I doing wrong? Where am I failing? I tried harder and harder and harder until I ended up in the hospital. I mean I just got carted out one night in a raving, screaming, manic fit. And I thought they were taking me to a mental institution which is . . . because I felt that I had lost my mind, that I just tried so hard that I just couldn't think or feel anything. But it turned out to be just a regular hospital.

Int.: How old was Heather then?

Mother: When I went to the hospital she was three months old.

Int.: You were in for how long?

Mother: For about 48 hours. When I came home my husband stayed home for three days and then we went away for about 5 days, up in the mountains someplace just camping. My mother watched the baby. And that did help some.

Int.: But you felt better when you heard about the Turner's. . . .

Mother: Yes. Yes. I didn't need a week off. I needed to know what was wrong with my baby. And it was like everyone was deceiving me and it made me . . . I had . . . it only gave me a few choices: I'm insane . . . I'm utterly incompetent . . . you know, I mean if the baby is all right and we're having all this trouble, what choices does it leave? So finally they said, you're right—your baby is a mess. I mean, you know, her chromosomes are screwed up. And it was a tremendous relief. I was very grateful to the doctor, I love her to this day. The doctor told me when Heather was three years old that things were worse than she thought. We went up and down and up and down. At first it was Turner's Syndrome. Children with Turner's Syndrome go to regular school. They're in the slow reading group, they're small. But that means if they are a year behind, it doesn't show. They make it. I mean when you think of what average is, it's not much of a goal. It's pretty easy to make. I mean average is waitress and truck driver. Well why shouldn't my child at least make that with hard work, be what these people are with no effort? Then when she was older, it didn't look so good. It looked like maybe she was trainable, or educable, but really retarded. She couldn't go to regular school. Then when she got older, well we don't see her as educable, but see her as possibly trainable. And then when she was three years old . . . you see we came down, down, down. . . . They told me it was Turner's Syndrome, but they told me it didn't mean a heck of a lot. That she would be slow, she'd be slow. But it wasn't going to be anything horrible. It wasn't until she was three that the doctor said: it does not look good. She is very severely retarded. She will be lucky to be semi-independent. I don't know whether she will ever make it to "city school" (the one public school for trainable retarded children in San Francisco)—I mean that is bad news. That's bad news. That was a much tougher thing to take. I came home, really, . . . I didn't cry when the doctor told me, I just looked at her. I said, I see. Yes, doctor. I see. I understand. And I went home and stormed and cried. That I guess was really the announcement for me. And, um, she told me then that she told me I should put Heather's name on the waiting list at the Pre-school. It's a very long list, it takes over a year, maybe she won't need it, maybe she'll be beyond that stage. But maybe she will need it. Maybe she won't be up to it, at four. But it looks like—you know, they're pretty permissive and tolerant there, and as long as the child is ambulatory they take him. And Heather was already showing signs of trying to walk. Anyhow, somebody on the staff took it upon themselves to do it for me. And they did call me and tell us we were on the waiting list. And it took about 14 months for her name to . . . it is a long list. Thank God I was put on. I'm grateful for . . . to the doctor, if she walked in this room, I'd fall down and kiss her feet. I adore the woman.

A sequel to this account is that six months after this interview, the child was re-evaluated at another medical center, where studies revealed she did not have Turner's Syndrome. Indeed it now seems she has no chromosomal abnormalities at all. The mother is now in the process of trying to reorient her past, present and future with respect to this latest professional opinion.

The last parent had this to say:

Mother: Well, I can tell you one thing—we did not know at birth that Christopher was mongoloid. We did not know until he was six months old. And it seemed that when he was born he very definitely had mongoloid features, but the . . . and the doctor had told my husband this, but we didn't know what it meant. I really didn't know what a mongoloid child was. And my husband said, oh the doctor said there might be something wrong with his features. And when the doctor came in I asked him and he said, oh no, no problem, he'll be perfectly all right. So for 6 months . . . looking back, he was my fourth child, and his development was not the same as theirs. His development . . . he was a slow gainer and he wasn't a good eater, whereas all my other children had been. And looking back I should have realized. And I remember Christopher . . . noticing his tongue, how large it was. But then when he was 6 months old, they told us of the possibility that he might be mongoloid. And of course, we both completely went to pieces. After having three other children, you'd have thought we'd know more about it. We didn't. I didn't know what a mongoloid child was. I just had heard wild stories that they had a large head, but I didn't know anyone with a retarded child and had never been around anyone with a retarded child. So we immediately went to the library and got all the books that we could on the subject. And they were all old, old stuff and threw us into a complete tizzy. We felt that he may never walk. He had already rolled over, and his development was somewhat normal. And we thought we might have just a vegetable. We¹ both went into just a complete mental thing which I think I am sort of coming out of now, but my husband isn't. He is not aware of this, but he really isn't. He has never been the same since. And then we went through the chromosome business to determine whether . . . that's how close he was to being normal. And we had to have that done three different times before it took. So we didn't know until Christmas. He was almost a year old. We got the good news Christmas Eve day that he was a mongoloid.

Int.: The original doctor didn't discuss with you . . .

Mother: No. And he was a family doctor, we'd had him for many years and . . . when Christopher was four months old we joined a health plan and the doctor there immediately recognized the features and he did not tell me. Then Christopher started this wheezing business and his eye turned in, and then finally at 6 months, he's the one that told us. And so I went back to the original doctor and he said, well even if he is, don't . . . ah, he might be just a little slower, don't be too worried about it. So we went from one extreme to another. His approach was quite different than the doctor at the health plan clinic. . . . Christopher got out on us one night—all six of us were in the house and we swore that somebody kidnapped him and called the police, he was gone maybe 45 minutes, and he had just wandered off and the police already had him by the time I called in. But that was like 20 years that he was gone. So this was at the point that I told my older children. They did not know, at this time, about Christopher.

Int.: How old was he then?

Mother: This was just about a year ago. Yeah, a year ago June, or something like that, (at which time the child was four) . . . the pediatrician had kept urging me to tell the other children, to tell the other children. But I felt this had to come from me.

Int.: How long was it before he suggested it—do you remember? Was he after you for a while for that?

Mother: Yes it seemed that every time I saw him with Christopher he mentioned that I tell the children. At this time I also had my father who had a long lengthy fatal illness and I knew he could not have accepted it. And I knew if he knew about Christopher that would be the end—Christopher was 20 months old when he passed away, so he died without knowing and this was another reason why I held off. And then having not discussed it with my mother, and then I thought well in a few months when she's over . . . and then I was pregnant with another baby. And then I didn't want to tell her then because I thought she'd worry for the next 9 months to see if it would happen again. It was a long drawn out, nerve-racking process before I did finally get to tell anybody, or felt that I could discuss it with anybody.

Int.: How did you feel about that . . . , that you were pregnant soon after? Did you wonder about whether or not your next child would. . . .

Mother: Yes I did. They told me not to be overly concerned, but there was never . . . but I was never given any reason why Christopher was born—they could find no medical reason. I had the chromosome test when I was pregnant with the baby and they found no hereditary factor involved; the fact that I wouldn't be a carrier, I was too young for, you know, the menopause. They said it was just a freak accident, so I thought it could happen again, but I tried to keep very calm and cool during the whole pregnancy. Of course we had been advised not to have any more children. . . .

Int.: That must have been quite a strain.

Mother: Yeah, that was quite a strain.

Int.: How did your husband feel?

Mother: I don't think he's accepted it yet. My husband is

a very deep man and keeps most of his thoughts to himself. He doesn't believe in showing emotion. And this has hit him harder than he realizes himself. And his behavior has changed a great deal not only to me, but many others have seen it in him. My husband doesn't see it in himself. He just thinks, you know, this is the way he is. But there's been a drastic change in his personality.

Int.: What kinds of things as you think back do you wish you had known, or maybe some help that you wish you could have gotten from other parents in the same boat or professionals who could have talked to you about it. For example you said you got a hold of some old books . . .

Mother: Well, I wish I could have read some up-dated literature with not such a pessimistic attitude. I also took him out to Chidren's Clinic, I guess he was a year old, or a year and a half old and they were very pessimistic in their approach. I was quite disappointed. I had him out there twice and I'm not going back there. They just feel that mongoloid children have a certain limitation and that's it. And I was very depressed when I left there both times. Yeah, they can reach a certain development and then forget it. And I don't feel that way. I mean we accept the fact that he's never going to be a genius or a normal child. He'll always live in a sheltered environment, but if we achieve that much, I'll be very grateful. One of the greatest things that bothered me was reading that they had such a short life expectancy. Now this completely cracked me up and now I find that this isn't true. I mean his heart and his vital organs seem to be normal. And that is the only good thing I heard out at the clinic. . . . And at this time (following the clinic experience) I badly needed spiritual advice and I didn't get any there, (from the church). And this was the greatest thing in my own mental develo . . . you know, the extent of the advice I got was—well, "'is he baptised in case he dies?" And ah, you know, it didn't do much for me believe me. So I felt that I could have talked to someone more understanding.

Interviewer: Have you had any other encounters with the church?

Mother: No, after that I, I'd pretty well had it after that.

... And the priest who told me this happens to be a doctor of psychology also and has done a great deal of work with the "feeble minded" as he calls them, and I expected a great deal more from him; more in the way of comfort or something. And I had terrible guilt feelings, I guess because as I say he wasn't a wanted child and I felt well God punished me, or punished this child because of me. I mean I had all this turmoil, mental turmoil going on for a long, long time and I really needed some kind of spiritual help, so like I say this attitude I've kind of developed is . . . you know I have him and I love him and everybody else can go to hell. I mean this is sort of a protective thing I guess. . . .

Int.: How old was he when you went to see the priest?

Mother: I didn't go to see the priest about him, I went to see him about some other matter and while I was there I thought, well I got up my courage and I thought well I'll ask . . . and along the line of birth control also and of course he said, there's no reason to practice . . . if you have another one, it's just too bad. Like I say, I came home completely shattered.[6] And then after that pessimistic approach I got at the hospital, I really felt . . . you know, I have this baby and I'm on my own with him.

THE NATURE AND CONSEQUENCES OF DOCTOR-PARENT INTERACTIONS

The author believes that the above accounts constitute at least a partial answer to the question posed by Ehlers, i.e. why do mothers of retarded children not see physicians and psychologists as offering the "most helpful" services? They are also useful in understanding why some parents of retarded children do not return for professional help or, if they do, are very skeptical of its reliability or credibility.

It is true that parents sometimes "distort" or "block" information. However, it should be clear from the accounts that this is only one side of the issue. The practitioner must assume a good share of the responsibility for establishing what the parents see as a "credibility gap." Such a state of affairs is hardly conducive to the establishment of "basic trust"—a condition generally assumed therapeutically essential in the doctor-patient relationship. The reciprocal feedback so essential to a successful doctor-patient interaction was, in the opinion of most of the parents, conspicuously absent. Ehlers notes that not only do mothers not rank doctors as "most helpful," but there is a peculiar reluctance on the mothers' part to discuss why.[7] This does not speak well for the unfounded assumption that so many practitioners routinely make, i.e. that they have succeeded in "establishing rapport" between themselves and their patients. It seems that both the nursery school teachers and public health nurses were more successful than the doctors in this regard.[8]

The question arises: what is the position of the physician with respect to the accounts of the parents given above? This remains an unknown as far as the particular doctors involved in the transcribed accounts are concerned. We have seen from the transcriptions that the parents were reluctant to lodge complaints with the doctor at the time of an unsatisfactory encounter. Ehlers has pointed out the parents' reluctance to discuss their complaints after the fact with others.

However, when the author played an edited tape of the mothers' accounts to a group of doctors in a training class on mental retardation, their explanation for the inaccurate diagnoses, lack of information or misinformation that the parents claim to have received was attributed to one of two causes: a) the atypical "unbelievable" incompetence of the particular doctors involved, or b) the typical "blocking" or "distortion" of information on the part of the parents. Greatest emphasis was placed on the latter. In the case of "a," they all felt they could never have been so mistaken under similar circumstances as the doctors in question seem to have been, and since, in the case of "b," there was probably no remedy, because of the mother's psychological need to "rationalize" her otherwise intractable position, they felt that the accounts had little relevance to them. In brief, they found the tapes very interesting—not as they reflected upon the practice of clinicians, but rather as they reflected upon how parents tended to "block" or "distort" information. This restricted outlook on the part of the doctor is particularly unfortunate, as it tends to contribute only disruptive influences to the doctor-patient interaction at the very time a successful interaction is most needed.

In order to better understand the dynamics involved in this process, I believe there is a need at this point to introduce a more detailed analysis of the mothers' verbatim accounts. It is clear from the doctors' reactions to hearing them on tape that here, as in so many other instances, the data do not speak for themselves. We have already mentioned the way in which doctors tended to presume against the accounts of the parents and how, from the clinicians' point of view, they needed to be ever vigilant for "blocking," "distortion," "selective perception," "projection," "resistance," and so many other pitfalls the expert is subject to in accepting the patient's accounts at face value.

With this in mind, one cannot help but wonder why evaluation teams, i.e. social workers, psychiatrists and psychologists, placed so much emphasis upon getting as detailed a "history" as possible in order to better understand family psychodynamics as well as the interaction they themselves engage in with the patients. There was an implicit understanding from the outset that these accounts were not to be taken seriously as they related to parents' recollections of factual information, observations, or sequential ordering of events. Yet it was on the basis of these accounts that the clinician was to "understand" the patient, i.e. interpret what the patient said of his current condition in the light of his past experience. As a result the clinician could not reject out of hand everything the patient told him. There was, for the clinician as for the patient, a selective perception at work whereby he tended to accept those segments of the account that supported his own position and to reject as distortion those aspects that did not. This says nothing, of course, of the "distortion" that the clinician introduces into the history. Doctors are the first to acknowledge that "they are only human"; "to be human is to err." Then, too, there are also the doctor's psychological needs and defenses which help him to cope with the patient. Yet little is ever said of the role of these contributing factors in the success or failure of the doctor-patient interaction.

These were only some of the ways in which the doctor contributed to the establishment of "communication problems." There

were many others. For example, there is the account of the first
mother who tells us: "Most doctors do not display their emotions
on their faces. . . ." This is for the most part a function of the
objective dispassionate observer that the doctor is supposed to
represent under the subset "scientist." Many therapies also consider it therapeutic for the doctor not to become "actively involved" with the patient. The patient, on the other hand, is
encouraged to display affect.

The consequence of this is that the doctor enjoys a feedback
of intelligence in the form of nonverbal communication that the
patient is denied. Then, too, it is the patient who gives the doctor
a history but never the other way around. In short, the position
of the patient with respect to receiving verbal and nonverbal cues
from the doctor is one of "relative deprivation." ". . . there was
an intern in the room, and there were several student nurses and
of course they're all saying, how cute, and I kept saying he's not
as cute as my first was, you know. (Indeed, she had already seen
his "puffy eyes" and "thrusting tongue.") The doctor still didn't
say anything you know." Finally, the doctor came to her to tell
her that her child was a mongoloid but it was she who had to
tell him. ". . . that poor doctor couldn't bring himself to say the
word." Imagine the mother's feelings at that point, when the
thing the doctor had come to relate to her about her recent crea-
tion was so horrendous that he was unable to speak the word.

Following this the question was raised as to whether or not
the baby was "really" mongoloid. Tests and X-rays were ordered
to make certain. The exact results of these and their implications
were never made known to the mother. This led her to say,
". . . I still maintain that doctors only tell you what they want
you to know, because I snuck a look at the X-ray report one
day in the pediatrician's office several months afterwards and
the diagnosis was, well the skull—one side showed the mongoloid
deformity and the other side didn't. And the navel zones were
normal and the pelvis, one side was normal and one side was
mongoloid degree, or whatever it is. And so the diagnosis was
'possible mongoloid'. . . ." The seeds of doubt were now sown and
the credibility gap opened. From that point on, it was for the

mother a question of—what else didn't they tell me?—and the
beginning of a belief in "you never can tell."

Next, the doctor told her that private homes were very costly
and that it wasn't easy to have a mongoloid child institutionalized.
This after she had "practically screamed at him" that she couldn't
bear to take the baby home. This was followed by the doctor
stating that he was unable to tell the mother "anything of how
the baby is going to develop . . ." because he just didn't know.
At this point she asked him if there was any literature or anything she could read, i.e. some way to find out something about
mongoloids that the doctor was unable or unwilling to tell her, to
which the doctor replied: "No, there is nothing." It is perhaps
not surprising that she and her husband were like "zombies" that
night, or that if they had had half a chance, "we would have
dumped him (the baby) in a garbage can." The next day, things
had not improved; in fact, the mother thought she "could take
this child home and smother it and they would attribute it to
a crib death."

Considering the nature and sequence of the doctor's statements on the preceding day, she was hardly left with a more
"adaptive" alternative. One ought not dismiss the above statements as "fantasies" on the basis of the fact that she did not
after all murder the child. There were at least two things in the
mother's account that seemed to have mitigated against this. First
was the "deus ex machina" telling her "listen lady . . . you don't
know what the child is going to be like." Secondly, as a result of
this, she felt compelled to "at least give him half a chance," which
is to say, ". . . at least . . . try to do what I'm supposed to." In-
dications are that the doctor's honesty in stating he did not know
how the child would develop, i.e. his establishing a problematic
future for the child, may have been inadvertently responsible
for saving the child's life. However, this does not excuse the doctor
for putting the child's life in jeopardy in the first place through
his inept handling of what was for him an unpleasant and for the
mother and child a potentially dangerous situation. Persons assuming the role of doctor ought to be able to bring themselves "to
say the word" and in such a crisis situation, really "know what
to say" and how to say it.

In a sense, it is perhaps not surprising to find that doctors don't know what to say. It is not a key part of medical curriculums to train and sensitize doctors to "non-medical" problems of this kind, even though it is known in advance that they are certain to encounter them. It is clear that more emphasis needs to be placed by medical schools upon this aspect of the doctor's projected career. It is clear that his inept handling of critical situations of this kind can have serious consequences for both the patient and his immediate family.

It would be too lengthy an undertaking to analyze each of the five accounts previously given within the limits of this chapter. Consequently the author will offer for the reader's consideration a final analysis. The reader will recognize, upon a careful reading of the remaining accounts, that although they duplicate certain forms of interactions found in the first two, which resulted in an unsatisfactory encounter between doctor and parent, they also introduce new forms of interactions not found there.

Let us consider now the account of the second parent who had this to say: "He was born premature and at the age of 3 months he had meningitis. And as far as anyone knows, the meningitis is what has retarded him. It's not a fact. It's just a theory, that's what they think. They don't know that he wasn't born like this. . . ." In her opening statement, the mother tells us that the child is retarded but it is uncertain why or how he got that way. She goes on to say in the first paragraph that in the course of trying to find out during the first six years of his life, ". . . the nicest thing that ever happened was getting him to come out to the pre-school, because until then we just got kind of shuffled back and forth from one place to another."

What the mother means by this becomes clear from what follows. The gist of it is that she went from one place to another seeking help and encountered one of two conditions: evaluations were made whose findings were not revealed to her, or, if certain findings were revealed, they were not explained. This was coupled with a series of dire predictions by physicians regarding the child's future that proved erroneous. For example, she was led to believe that the child would not survive the meningitis, that he was deaf, and later that he would be unable to walk or would only walk with crutches. The outcomes were: the child lived, his hearing is fine, and he walks (although unevenly) without the aid of crutches. In describing these encounters, the mother put it this way:

> We had ordered a psychological evaluation on Eric and they told me they had set up a date for it and had ordered it and so I took Eric and had his evaluation and that was the last I heard of it, except when I got billed for $17.50. I never heard anything from it. Nothing. And that was my biggest complaint about the situation; everytime you ask a question, you're answered with a question. There's no, there's no facts given. And I don't think it's really fair because when you go into this, it's new, it's never happened to you before, and you don't know what to expect, you don't know which way to turn or where to go.

Not only is the cause of the retardation unknown, but its significance in terms of a prognosis remains very ambiguous for the mother.

> *Int.*: Was one of the things you were worrying about, thinking about then, how much Eric would develop and how far you could expect him to go and what to expect of him?
>
> *Mother*: Right. We still don't know. We just go from day to day and I assume he will talk eventually because he does have speech. He does say "ma ma." He can say "no." His speech is there, but how much he will ever talk is another question too that there's no answer to.

Given Eric's developmental pattern and current status, the prognosis is poor. However, if the mother is skeptical of the professional opinion, she does have grounds.

> ". . . We were also told he wouldn't walk, (she might have added "live" or "hear") and he walks now. So we just are patient now, and I'm sure he'll say something eventually, when, that's another thing. Of course that's something you can't do anything about. You just have to wait for it."

The mother's position may be summarized as one of skepticism of professional opinions for two reasons: 1) they have proved systematically inaccurate, and 2) they have been of little or no assistance in reversing her child's condition. Waiting patiently for her child to talk is only one thing "you can't do anything about," i.e. only one thing the coming of which the professionals are unable to predict or assist in. This, in conjunction with other predictions noted above, has led this mother to avoid doctors' opinions, evaluations and/or reevaluations. She now seeks professional help only in the case of serious physical illness which neither she nor her child has experienced for the past few years. In short, she sees the doctor now only when she feels she has no choice and never in regard to her child's current status or future expectations,

One of the things that led to her skepticism was a factor previously dealt with, i.e. the doctor's reluctance to take her evaluation of her child's condition seriously.

> ". . . my doctor went under the assumption that he (Eric) was deaf; for the simple reason that in 90% of the cases of meningitis that he had been affiliated with, deafness was the handicap that was left. So he assumed that Eric's slowness was because he was deaf. And after Eric was about a year old we kept insisting that he could hear. We kept insisting that he could hear, he could hear. And finally when he was two, the doctor understood that Eric could hear. We got a radio out and turned it on and he knew then. . . . Well of course when he had the hearing tests and the hearing tested out fine, he told me maybe we weren't quite so lucky. . . . Because when it wasn't the hearing, it was mental."

Apart from not acknowledging her evaluation of her child's condition (an evaluation that proved correct when the doctor's proved wrong), the implications of other prognoses made by the professional (apart from the fact that they proved inaccurate) were not explained to her. For example:

Mother: Well, we had consultations and it just seems like it's one big series of questions, questions, questions, questions. And the doctor said that . . . the last time I spoke with her that . . . which was after the evaluation, that Eric would never walk, that he would probably walk with crutches, but that he wouldn't be able to walk and that we would have to be prepared to find permanent care of Eric. And she, at the time, did not elaborate on. . . .

Int.: . . . where or how or . . .

Mother: . . . or how much, or anything like that. And of course I have Eric with me most of the time. By the time you get through getting questioned, you're ready to go home. And there's really nothing definite, no. So we just go from one place to the next and from one day to the next. It's just such . . . nothing is down in black and white.

In other instances, the findings with respect to the child's evaluation were not only not explained but were not even revealed to her.

Mother: I know he's had an EEG, but what that showed— there was never anything done, my own doctor finally told me that if they ever decided to do another one that it wouldn't show anything only that Eric had an abnormal brain pattern. But other than that, it wouldn't show anything. So it's just been more or less a matter of somebody throwing you in the water and you just have to learn to swim, that's what it is. It's an awful, awful thing because it seems like you're just never going to find your way out of it, this maze that you're in.

Before going on to consider some other forms of doctor-patient interactions, the reader is cautioned not to view the above accounts as being somehow peculiar to the fourteen mothers in the author's series. They are not. The following are a few examples taken from the parents in Kramm's series.

"We know the doctor couldn't prevent the child from being mongoloid but he could have taken at least five minutes to explain."

"I later asked a friend what mongolism meant. She looked the word up in the dictionary, then told me Beth was just like a mongrel dog. I felt so terrible I cried."

"Our family doctor . . . told us the child wasn't normal but he wouldn't say what was wrong. We had to pump him. Finally when my husband asked him if there was something wrong with the child's brain the doctor said yes, but he wouldn't tell us what was wrong until after returning from his vacation three weeks later. During those three weeks we concluded ourselves that the baby was mongoloid. I feel the doctor's attitude was bad. He didn't even give the normal support any doctor would give a new mother. He said the baby would probably die in a year anyway. He lost complete interest in him."

"The doctor was blunt. He didn't seem to want to talk. All he said was, 'It is my personal observation that the child is mongoloid.' My head swam. I fell backwards, gasping."

"The very next day after his birth they told me that he was a mongoloid and that there was nothing to do except to put him in an institution. On the eighth day two other doctors, one in the afternoon and one in the evening, examined David and confirmed the diagnosis. The one in the afternoon said, 'He's going to be retarded all his life and there's nothing you can do about it.' The one in the evening said, 'He has all the symptoms of mongolism and there is nothing left for you to do but put him in an institution.' The other doctor gave me no encouragement whatsoever. It was the blunt curtness of his response to my questions that hurt. When I would ask questions like, 'When will he sit up?' he would reply shortly, 'I don't know if he'll ever sit up.' It was that sort of thing that got me. When I took David in for his first six-week check-up, the pediatrician never told me how he was progressing or expressed interest. He merely undressed him, looked at him, said he'd always be sickly and susceptible to pneumonia. So what was I supposed to do, hang David on a tree because he was susceptible to pneumonia! I simply dreaded the six-week check-ups."

A key factor in the unfavorable encounters that parents of retarded children experienced with physicians related directly to the fact that they were unable to acquire from the physician a more or less satisfactory presentation and evaluation of their child's current condition and future expectations. Apart from the parent's "blocking," "distorting," "resisting" or "projecting," their failure to acquire a satisfactory diagnosis may be attributed to one or more of the following causes: 1) there were certain problems in communication between the doctor and parents, so that a diagnosis was made but was not explained or adequately explained to the parent, who was then left to his own resources to interpret it; 2) there occurred a series of diagnoses and prognoses from doctors, some or all of which proved false, resulting in the parents' feeling that they could no longer take the professional's evaluation of their child's condition seriously; 3) certain information related to the diagnosis was withheld from parents, or not infrequently, the diagnosis itself was withheld; 4) the doctor, while confident in diagnosing the child as retarded, was unable to attribute the retardation to any specific known cause, leaving the parent with an ambiguous situation that provided for both hope and frustration at the same time[10]; 5) a diagnosis of mental retardation was made that later proved "false," e.g. the child was early diagnosed as "severely retarded" and at some later point in time appeared normal; in such instances, it was invariably assumed that there was an inaccurate diagnosis in the first place, since the professional's current perspective provides that retardation, and especially severe retardation, is irreversible.

CURRENT OUTLOOKS AS SELF-FULFILLING PROPHECIES

We have already seen examples of four of these causes of parental distress in the verbatim accounts of the mothers previously given. The following discussion will offer an example of the fifth and last of the causes noted above. This form of parental distress resulted to a large extent from the clinician's traditional outlook toward mental retardation and his routine acceptance of this outlook as "given." The initiation and perpetuation of this outlook is in turn very much influenced by the fact that most of the research and training funds spent on mental retardation are kept within medical settings. Most of these funds are used in the search for biochemical, genetic or organic causes of retardation. Much of the remaining money goes to the search for psychiatric and psychological explanations. Very little of these funds filters down for the study and/or prevention and treatment of mental retardation on a social, educational, or rehabilitational level. Albee had this to say regarding the existing priorities used to allocate mental retardation funds:

I believe, . . . that it is not only unfair, but unreasonable that almost every new federally funded, university-affiliated center to train people and to engage in research in this field is in a medically dominated and bio-medically oriented center. Even in the Mental Retardation Research Centers being funded by the new National Institute of Child Health and Human Development, the major efforts are bio-medical. Instead, at least half of these centers should be designed for research in special educational methods and rehabilitation; others should be designed primarily for research in the social and behavioral-science approaches to helping the retarded. . . .

Why is the emphasis, both in research and in treatment, on organic approaches to retardation? One reason: the academic mental institutions' insatiable need for research money. Because of the enormous Federal funds recently made available for constructing research and training facilities in the area of retardation, medicine—particularly psychiatry and pediatrics—has discovered and promulgated compelling arguments why these research centers should be placed in medical settings. Almost exclusive emphasis has been on all of the external causes of retardation—the metabolic, the infections, the undiscovered causes of brain damage. In addition, by controlling the advisory committees that rule on applications for construction funds to build the university-affiliated facilities, the doctors have controlled the character of these centers still further. . . . According to the President's Panel, a very large majority of the retarded can, with special training and assistance, acquire limited job skills and achieve a high measure of independence; they represent 85 percent of the retarded group. . . . State vocational agencies that provide urgently-needed vocational rehabilitation for the mildly retarded are currently reaching only 3 percent of them. . . . The truth is that most retardation is *not* an inherited disease. Quite correctly, President Kennedy's Panel on Mental Retardation emphasized the fact that '. . . about 75 percent to 85 percent of those now diagnosed as retarded show no demonstrable gross brain abnormality. They are, by and large, persons with relatively mild degrees of retardation. . . . Unfavorable environmental and psychological influences are thought to play an important contributory role among this group. Such influences include interference with normal emotional and intellectual stimulation in early infancy, unfavorable psychological or emotional experiences in early childhood, and lack of normal intellectual and cultural experiences during the entire developmental period.' . . . A large percentage of urban indigent Negro mothers are 'walk-ins' who receive little or no prenatal care, no special instructions on diets, and no medical guidance until labor pains begin. The retardation rate in infants born to these indigent mothers is ten times the white rates.[11]

The gulf between the medical and sociological outlooks on mental retardation can be put in sharp relief by comparing the positions of Doll and Perry respectively.

1. In the light of present knowledge, mental retardation is irreversible. This does not deny the possibility of prevention or amelioration; but though many therapies and other maneuvers have been hailed, few have survived the test of time. Preventive measures . . . have had some limited success; but *adequately diagnosed mental retardation probably never is reversed to normal.*[12] (Emphasis added)

2. Mental retardation ". . . requires a complete reassessment of the nature of mental deficiency. . . . Each mentally defective person must be considered, not as belonging to a homogeneous category called deficiency, but as an individual; his subnormal intellectual functioning must be considered, not as constitutionally or organically determined, but as an interdependent complex of constitutional or physiological processes, interpersonal processes, and sociocultural processes; and from a research standpoint

the mentally defective must be approached, *not with an assumption of irreversibility and permanence, but with the assumption that benevolent intervention may lead to a reversibility or improvement of the conditions.*"[13] (Emphasis added)

While the former view has currently gained general acceptance among practitioners, the latter is not without precedent. Itard, in undertaking the education and socialization of the "Wild Boy of Aveyron," held a similar view. He proposed that social deprivation might not only be the cause of mild retardation (a view currently more and more in vogue) but of severe retardation as well. Furthermore, he felt that this state might not only be prevented but, once incurred, it might also be reversed.

> If it were proposed to solve the following problem of metaphysics; to *determine what would be the degree of intelligence and the nature of the ideas of an adolescent, who, deprived from his childhood of all education, had lived entirely separated from individuals of his own species,* unless I am greatly mistaken the solution of the problem would be found as follows. There should first be assigned to that individual nothing but an intelligence relative to the small number of his needs and one which was deprived, by abstraction, of all the simple and complex ideas we receive by education, which combine in our mind in so many ways solely by means of our knowledge of signs, or reading. Well, the mental picture of this adolescent would be that of the Wild Boy of Aveyron. . . .[14]
>
> This is what appeared to me to be the cause of his present state. It can be seen why I argued favorably from it for the success of my treatment. Indeed, considering the short time he was among people, the Wild Boy of Aveyron was much less an adolescent imbecile than a child of ten or twelve months, and a child who would have the disadvantage of antisocial habits, a stubborn inattention, organs lacking in flexibility and a sensibility accidentally dulled. . . .[15]

Itard recommended as a means of arresting and reversing this process five principle aims for the "mental and moral education of the Wild Boy of Aveyron."

1st Aim. To interest him in social life by rendering it more pleasant to him than the one he was then leading, and above all more like the life which he had just left.

2nd Aim. To awaken his nervous sensibility by the most energetic stimulation, and occasionally by intense emotion.

3rd Aim. To extend the range of his ideas by giving him new needs and by increasing his social contacts.

4th Aim. To lead him to the use of speech by inducing the exercise of imitation through the imperious law of necessity.

5th Aim. To make him exercise the simplest mental operations upon the objects of his physical needs over a period of time, afterwards inducing the application of these mental processes to the objects of instruction.[16]

The author believes that these aims might still well serve as a model program for dealing with the problems of mental retardation. Itard's pioneering effort and the elaborate descriptions he left of his "experiments" with the Wild Boy of Aveyron offer a valuable handbook for those dealing with the mentally retarded. Some indication of how popular this perspective is and the extent to which those in the field avail themselves of this resource (the numerous casual references to Itard found in the literature notwithstanding) is the fact that not one single copy of this work was available in the library of one of the largest medical centers in the country. So strong is the clinician's current commitment to Doll's position that there is little or no prospect of reversing "adequately diagnosed" mental retardation to a normal or above-normal level of intelligence, that its reversibility to normality is never entertained, let alone accepted, the contrary evidence notwithstanding.

One example of such evidence is the case of non-verbal non-testable children diagnosed severely retarded and/or schizophenic. In such cases, when no organic pathology can be established (in fact, the "etiology" usually remains unknown), the question arises as to whether the child is retarded, schizophrenic or both. This provides the clinician with a difficult diagnostic problem. Such children are often considered brain-damaged at one clinic, schizophrenic at another and both at a third with an emphasis on one or the other. One expert had this to say about this class of children and their prospects for a definitive diagnosis:

> ... the diagnostic schizophrenia that exists in many states—in this commonwealth, for example, where certified psychiatrists in one institution claim a patient is primarily retarded, whereas in another they say, with the same conviction, that the person is primarily psychotic or mentally ill, making an individual patient a virtual football between two teams of experts. The commissioner in the state house usually referees these games.[17]

The ambiguity surrounding this sub-average level of intellectual performance of these children is not surprising. Among those who consider the child schizophrenic or autistic, there arises the question of whether these are the same or distinct entities.[18] Apart from whether or not they are the same, there is the prior question of what they are.

> In planning such corrective remediation, the therapist inevitably assumes a theory of etiology though it is most often more implicit than explicit. . . . Indeed, one must not lose sight of the additional fact that the descriptive entity childhood schizophrenia is grossly defined and differences among the children within any schizophrenic sample are as striking as are the similarities. Certainly the notion of a disease in the sense of a single definable pathologic agent remote in time, an inevitable course of development, and a predetermined course of treatment is still a mythical one.[19]

On the other hand, those who attribute the child's sub-average intellectual performance to some organic pathology not infrequently infer its existence on the basis of "clinical insight," since in the above cases no organicity is in evidence. In fact, it is generally true that given the ambiguity surrounding the etiology, the diagnosis given children exhibiting the above symptoms is, in any particular case, likely to favor the orientation of the particular agency for which the clinician works.

These problems are compounded by certain other distinctions and assumptions routinely made by practitioners in such cases.

For example, depending upon the agency, a distinction is sometimes drawn between "functional retardation" and "mental deficiency." Functional retardation refers to the fact that the child
is performing at a sub-average level of intelligence. It is usually
inferred, with a diagnosis of "functional retardation," that the
child may possess the potential to perform at a much higher level
of intelligence (perhaps at a normal or above-normal level) but
is unable to do so because of severe emotional problems. Schizophrenic children are usually diagnosed "functionally retarded."
The diagnosis of "mental deficiency," while it also refers to a
sub-average intellectual performance, implies the child does not
have the potential to perform at a substantially higher level because of some real or inferred "organicity." In short, there is some
hope that those who are "functionally retarded" may find their
retardation "reversed," since they were not "really" retarded in
the first place, while those who are "mentally deficient" are given
no hope of ever achieving a normal level of intelligence.

Notwithstanding the general acceptance of the above assumptions, the author has presented, in a previous work, detailed case
history material which places the validity of these assumptions
in question.[20] Among the cases of non-verbal non-testable children with no demonstrable organic pathology, there are instances
of children "adequately diagnosed" as "severely retarded" (deficient) relatively late in childhood who are later found to function
at a normal or above-normal level of intelligence. In such cases of
miraculous recovery, it is invariably held that the original diagnosis (even when rendered by a qualified licensed psychiatrist
and supported by the child's developmental history) was a case of
misdiagnosis and that the child was not severely retarded but
schizophrenic. However, it is not assumed of the infrequent cases
of children recovering from childhood schizophrenia that they
might have recovered from mental retardation instead or as well.

There are good grounds on which to question the routine
acceptance of these assumptions. An alternative hypothesis and
one given by the author is that one's intellectual potential may be
missing at one point (i.e. the child was at the time of the original
diagnosis in fact severely retarded), and be recovered or acquired

for the first time at some later point. In short, there is every indication that adequately diagnosed retardation, indeed severe retardation, is reversible, at least in some cases for the class of children described above.

The author believes that clinicians, upon hearing cases of "miraculous recovery" presented, would have quite naturally favored the author's position were it not for the fact that they were previously committed to the outlook that all "adequately diagnosed" retardation is irreversible to a normal or above-normal level of intelligence. Until more is known about the course and causes of mental retardation (the literature now notes from 100[21] to 200 "causes"[22]), it would be well to accept Perry's more cautious position, given the serious implications for diagnosis and treatment of prematurely accepting the assumptions of Doll's hypothesis as "given."

The reader is cautioned not to view the above discussion as "academic." The fact is that the consequences of a child receiving a diagnosis of "severe functional retardation" (as in the case of childhood schizophrenia) as opposed to a diagnosis of "severe mental deficiency" are very real. In the first case, some hope is held out for his eventual recovery, even to his achieving a normal or above normal level of intelligence. As such, he may receive a good deal of attention and an active course of treatment. On the other hand, the child given the diagnosis of "severe mental deficiency" is given little or no hope for recovery and is likely to receive little or no effort towards an effective program of treatment. The author suggests that in light of the evidence a reevaluation of the general acceptance of this position is long overdue. Each case ought to be considered individually and on its own merits, as Perry suggests, until more is known about the general conditions of "mental retardation."

There are other problems of outlook in the field of mental retardation that result in ambiguous diagnosis and other problems for the parent seeking help. Perhaps the most ubiquitous of these are "intelligence tests." Mental retardation is generally defined "operationally" in terms of I.Q. The American Association on Mental Deficiency states that:

. . . Mental retardation refers to subaverage intellectual functioning which originates during the development period and is associated with impairment in adaptive behavior.[23]

Adaptive behavior includes social skills, as well as level of intellectual functioning. A convenient standardized quantitative measure of social skills, on which there is some consensus, is still forthcoming.[24] Retardation is more frequently dealt with in terms of I.Q. test scores. One system of categorization widely employed is that of the American Association on Mental Deficiency. Five categories are used to indicate a range of subnormal intellectual functioning, i.e. borderline (I.Q. 70-84), mildly retarded (I.Q. 55-69), moderately retarded (I.Q. 40-54), severely retarded (I.Q. 25-39), and profoundly retarded (I.Q. 0-24). This expedient also requires a number of arbitrary designations to be made.

Gladwin has this to say about the universal unfounded and confounded use of intelligence tests as a convenient means of defining and recognizing mental retardation:

But a far more severe stumbling block (to the study of change and development of intelligence) is created by intelligence tests, one of which is not only not diminishing appreciably, but is scarcely even being attacked. This lies in the fact that we really do not know what intelligence tests measure. The corollary to this is that we do not know, and are making little effort to find out, what intelligence is. In the last analysis intelligence is defined for practical purposes as being what intelligence tests measure. Since different tests will often produce different I.Q.'s we arrive at the absurd point of different kinds of intelligence without knowing whether any difference really makes a difference, since we do not know what we are measuring. Yet we have been chasing our tails around in this circle for so long that we seem to take it for granted that this is a reasonable way to function. . . .[26]

In considering the mental abilities required for satisfactory school performance we must also consider that required for intelligence test performance. Present-day intelligence tests, and even performance tests, appear to be quite unreliable in predicting social and occupational adequacy outside of the school situation. This is not surprising, for the early work of Binet and Terman and others in standardizing the first intelligence tests, against which practically all later tests are standardized, used school performance as the primary standardizing criterion. In other words, insofar as they predict anything, I.Q.'s predict only school performance, and in view of the manner of their construction we should not expect them to predict anything else. . . .[27]

If we put these facts together several things become clear. One is that, omitting the organic cases, we cannot do satisfactory research on mental retardation as it is usually defined, since this definition, whatever it may be, is variable, unreliable, and includes within it factors other than mental ability. Presumably we should confine our attention purely to mental ability and discard the community's fuzzy criteria for retardation. But, then we must ask, ability to do what? To perform in school, or to perform in the broader setting of our society? The data just cited make it obvious that these require different kinds of abilities, and failure in one does not necessarily mean failure in the other.[28]

Since one is considered retarded or not primarily on the basis of his I.Q. score, and since it has proved an extremely illusive task to establish what it is this score is a measure of (apart from a reasonable approximation of school performance), it might be better to re-evaluate the universal acceptance and use of I.Q. test scores in defining the degree of, or existence of, mental retardation. Professionals are not the only ones who use the term "retardation" loosely. Lay persons and other helping agents also share in this inexact and sometimes indiscriminate labeling process. A survey of persons under eighteen years of age in Onondaga County, New York, who were referred by people or agencies as "retarded," revealed that twenty-five percent of these for whom I.Q. scores were available had an I.Q. of 90 or over.[29] Then too, many persons defined as "mildly retarded" on the basis of school performance and/or I.Q. scores stop being retarded for all intents and purposes when they leave school, i.e. blend unobtrusively into the social fabric.[30] It might be better if retardation was seen in terms of one's sensitivity and adaptability to his social environment rather than in terms of substandard I.Q. test scores. The former by no means implies the latter.[31] It is true that a measure of social sensitivity and adaptability is not easily come by. However, it is no easier to measure intelligence, the "successful" and accepted application of "intelligence quotients" notwithstanding.

CONCLUSIONS

I have presented in this chapter some of the forms of interaction that parents and physicians participated in, why these took place, and why they resulted in unsatisfactory encounters from the parents' point of view. The nature of these encounters affected the careers of both parents and child, as well as the effectiveness of clinical programs designed to meet the needs of the retarded and their families. In concluding, I have considered some of the basic outlooks on and orientations toward mental retardation held by professionals and lay persons, and how these can affect the lives of patients and parents, as well as the effectiveness of the physicians' efforts. The case was also made for reordering existing priorities in mental retardation. The author feels greater emphasis should be placed upon educational and rehabilitation services, and social and behavioral science research. As things currently stand, far too much effort and money is being shunted into medical settings for research and treatment programs that benefit only a small percentage of the retarded.

FOOTNOTES—CHAPTER I

1. Walter H. Ehlers, *Mothers of Retarded Children: How They Feel, Where They Find Help.* Springfield, Illinois: Charles C Thomas, 1966, pp. 91-92.
2. This account was taken from a taped interview conducted two years prior to the author's study by a psychiatrist for the benefit of a group of medical students. The account is that of the father. The mother was one of the parents interviewed by the author. A comparison of the two accounts two years apart, particularly with respect to the child's developmental history, finds the two accounts to be very consistent. The tendency of physicians to discount parents' appraisals of their child's potential is particularly unfortunate, since these appraisals have very often proved to be accurate. See for example: G. Boles, "Personality Factors in Mothers of Cerebral

Palsied Children," *Genetic Psychology Monographs 1959*, pp. 159-218; Harriet L. Reingold, "Interpreting Mental Retardation to Parents," *Journal of Consulting Psychology*, 1945, 9. pp. 142-148.
3. Ehlers, *op cit.*, p. 59.
4. *Ibid.*, p. 79.
5. Elizabeth R. Kramm, *Families of Mongoloid Children.* Washington, D.C.: Children's Bureau, U. S. Department of Health, Education & Welfare, 1963, p. 8. For other examples of parental dissatisfaction with doctor-parent interactions, see: Charlotte H. Waskowitz, "The Parents of Retarded Children Speak for Themselves," *Journal of Pediatrics*, 1959, 54, pp. 319-329; J. Tizard and Jacqueline Grad, *The Mentally Handicapped and Their Families: A Social Survey.* London: Oxford University Press, 1961; R. A. Jensen, "The Clinical Management of the Mentally Retarded Child and the Parents," *American Journal of Psychiatry*, 1950, 106, pp. 830-833.
6. For a discussion of the Clergy's reluctance to accept the help of parents of retarded children in gaining some insight into the problems of counseling this group, see Harry Raech, "A Parent Discusses Initial Counseling," *Mental Retardation*, 4 (2), 1966, pp. 25-26.
7. Ehlers, *op. cit.*, p. 53.
8. *Ibid.*, pp. 51-54.
9. Kramm, *op. cit.*, pp. 8-10.
10. For an excellent discussion and examples of these forms of interactions, and the problems they generate, see Raech, *op. cit.*, pp. 25-26.
11. George W. Albee, "Needed: A Revolution in Caring for the Retarded," *Trans-Action*, 18, Jan.-Feb., 1968, pp. 2-7.
12. Edgar A. Doll, "Recognition of Mental Retardation in the School-Age Child," in Irving Philips (ed.), *Prevention and Treatment of Mental Retardation*, New York: Basic Books, 1966, p. 62.
13. Roy De Verl Willer and Kathleen Barnette Waite, *The Mentally Retarded Child*, Springfield, Illinois, Charles C Thomas, 1964, pp. 6-7.
14. Jean Marc-Gaspard Itard, *The Wild Boy of Aveyron.* New York: Century Company, 1932, p. 7.
15. *Ibid.*, pp. 10-11.
16. *Ibid.*
17. A statement by Dr. Peter Bowman, Superintendent, Pineland Hospital and Training Center, Maine, in the *CPMR Message*, No. 11, April 1968, p. 1.
18. Benjamin Pasamanick, "Etiologic Factors in Early Infantile Autism and Childhood Schizophrenia," *Journal of the Hillside Hospital*, 16(1), January, 1967, pp. 42-52.
19. William Goldfarb, "Corrective Socialization: A Rationale Treatment of Schizophrenic Children," *Journal of the Hillside Hospital*, 16(1), January 1967, pp. 58-71.
20. Jerry Jacobs, "The Social Organization of Mental Retardation Categories," in *Deviancy in American Society*, ed., by Jack D. Douglas, Basic Books (in press).
21. Robert B. Edgerton, *Cloak of Competence*, Berkeley: University of California Press, 1967, p. 2.

22. *Mental Retardation,* reprinted from the *Journal of the American Medical Association,* 191 (3), January 18, 1965, p. 1.
23. Edgerton, *op. cit.,* p. 3.
24. *Ibid.,* p. 3.
25. *Ibid.,* p. 5.
26. Thomas Gladwin, "Current Cultural and Psychological Research in Mental Retardation," *Regional Conference on Mental Retardation,* presented by the Illinois Department of Public Welfare and the U.S. Department of Health, Education and Welfare, 1958, p. 40.
27. *Ibid.,* p. 38.
28. *Ibid.,* p. 37.
29. *Ibid.,* p. 37.
30. Stewart E. Perry, "Notes for a Sociology of Prevention in Mental Retardation," in Irving Philips (ed.), *Prevention and Treatment of Mental Retardation,* New York: Basic Books, 1960, p. 163.
31. Edgerton, *op. cit.,* pp. 196-197.

CHAPTER II

Educating the Retarded: Programs and Prospects

CHAPTER I COVERED some of the encounters between parents of retarded children and physicians during the first stage of their search for help, as well as outlining some of the forms of interaction occasioned by these encounters. Let me begin a consideration of the second stage by offering a brief sketch of how the parents and children came to be launched upon their educational careers. I include the parents as well as the children, because the Pre-school has been for them, in their own words, "an education." This will be followed by a description of the parent and children groups, the Pre-school's program, and finally a discussion of educational outlooks and facilities for the retarded.

REFERRALS

Referrals to the Pre-school usually took one of the following forms. Parents were referred by professional persons (5), read about the Pre-school in a newspaper advertisement and were self-referred (3), or heard about the school through a spot radio announcement and were self-referred (1). The source of referral for five of the parents remains unknown.

An interesting feature of the way in which parents found out about the Pre-school, apart from the immediate "source of referral," was the fact that many discovered it on their own and/or through some fortuitous circumstance. For example, some "professional referrals" were instances of the doctor's only casually mentioning the Pre-school. It remained for the parent at that point "to pump the doctor" for more information. Had the parents missed their cue or otherwise failed to pursue the doctor's passing reference, they might never have learned of the Pre-school. The need for better informational and referral services was summed up by one parent as follows:

> I wish there were more current literature or that I could have talked to someone that knew more about it. And this was the hard thing. I had this child and I really didn't know where to go and I knew I badly needed help, both for myself and for him and we just kind of didn't know where to turn. . . . I found out just about everything on my own through the paper and now of course I understand there is a referral service. I'm becoming more and more aware of things.

The lack of information and/or the transfer of information regarding educational services for the retarded was not restricted to parents and physicians. Educational referral services were also sometimes found to be unreliable. One mother, who had been referred to the Pre-school by her pediatrician, gave this account:

Int.: How did you find out about this place?

Mother: My pediatrician . . . he said it's time for her to go to school, she just turned five in June (she was eligible at age four) and he said that, um, to look into some schools and he gave me two names (the only two facilities available in the area) . . . and I contacted both.

Int.: Did you know about this school or other kinds of . . .

Mother: Nothing.

Int.: You didn't know about it before your pediatrician mentioned it?

Mother: Nothing, not a thing, no.

Int.: Suppose he (the pediatrician) didn't know about it or didn't mention it? Do you think you would have kept Anna at home?

Mother: Oh yes . . . see I phoned up the Board of Education, and they said they didn't know of any place, the woman I didn't get her name, she said how old is the child, and I said she's five, and she said: call back in three years (The age range in the only public facility for "trainable" retarded children is from 8 to 18.). So I would have just phoned back in three years.

Some parents, even after they acquired the necessary information to apply to one or the other of these educational facilities, experienced a form of interaction not unlike that described in Chapter I under "Lack of Feedback" in doctor-patient interactions. The above mother gave this account:

> I sent a whole bunch of papers and I signed them all, to X school. And that gives them permission to go look at your income tax papers and you just name it. And that's still. . . . I never did hear about it. I thought maybe I would go up and, but you think they would have sent a card back saying, we have received your application or there was a waiting list, we have maybe so many on the waiting list, and it's a slow process so maybe she wouldn't be called for 1½ years, or she could be called within six months—no, nothing! Not a thing. That was it. They got all that information and everything. And I sent the whole batch of it in. I sent it in as soon as we went away (on a vacation) and then I sent the letter out there (on her return). And then that was it. (She never heard from the school again.)

Another parent had this to say about the ubiquitous influence of the lack of communication in contributing to her problems:

> I think the whole thing is just a matter of communication. And it's the lack of it that leaves you up in the air, because I think any person can cope with anything as long as they know what they're doing. As long as they know what they're up against. It's what you don't know and don't understand. . . .

While it is an oversimplification to say that "the whole thing" is a matter of communication, many of the problems the parents encountered resulted from a lack of communication between themselves and professionals. It is also true that the professional often played a key role in creating these problems —sometimes inadvertently, sometimes intentionally. I have dealt above with how parents became acquainted with the Pre-school and with some of their problems in the pre- and post-stages of the referral process. The reader has already gained some introduction to the parents and children, as individuals, through a reading of the verbatim accounts found in Chapter I. The following outline will present an overview of their group characteristics.

THE PARENT GROUP

Age: Mothers' ages ranged from 31 to 51, with a mean of 38. Six mothers were over the age of 40 at the time of their retarded child's birth. Fathers' ages ranged from 26 to 67 with a mean of 43.

Race: Of the 14 mothers interviewed, 12 were white and two were Negro.

Religion: Religious affiliations were given as follows: Eleven mothers were Catholic, two were Protestant, and one, Russian Orthodox. In three cases, the husband and wife held different religious affiliations.

Income: Net family incomes ranged from $327 to $1,000 per month. The average net family income was $650 per month.

Marital status: Thirteen of the 14 families in this series were intact. There was only one instance of a "broken home," i.e. an absent father. Eleven mothers had been married only once; three had been married twice. Of the fathers, eleven had married only once; two had been married twice.

Number of children: The number of children in the family unit ranged from one to ten, with an average of four. Nine of the 14 families had three or fewer children. All families had only one retarded child.

Residential mobility: All the families in this series showed considerable residential stability. All fourteen had lived in the San Francisco area since the birth of their retarded child, i.e. for the past four to eight years, often in the same house.

Employment: Eleven of the fourteen mothers in this series

were "housewives." At the time of the interview, only three
mothers were employed. Two of these were the only Negro parents
interviewed, and the third mother reported the only case of a
"broken home." One of the Negro mothers was employed with
the telephone company; the other worked in a laundry. The third
and only white working mother managed an apartment house. The
fathers worked at a wide variety of jobs. These occupations are
listed as follows: auto mechanic, house painter, longshoreman,
pharmacist, army colonel, public school teacher, shipping clerk
supervisor, retired limousine driver, mechanic's helper, lawyer,
city fireman, lather and state investigator.

Education: One mother had not graduated from high school,
six were high school graduates, and three had some college or
were college graduates. In four cases the level of mothers' education remains unknown. Of the fathers, three had not graduated
from high school, one graduated high school, and five had some
college or were college graduates. In four cases the level of
fathers' education was not given. In two cases, mothers claimed
they had never known the level of their husbands' education. It
seems it was a topic that never came up.

THE CHILDREN

Of the 14 children in the author's series, there were six males
and eight females ranging in age from 4 to 8, i.e. within the age
range accepted by the Pre-school. In terms of diagnostic categories, there were 10 mongoloids, one case of "Turner's Syndrome," one schizophrenic child, and one case of cerebral palsy
resulting from meningitis. While all the children at the Pre-school
were by definition "retarded," the prognosis—as we have already
seen from the prior accounts—was for many ambiguous at best. In
some cases even the diagnosis of mental retardation itself, as it
is commonly understood within the medical model, was questionable. Perhaps a more meaningful description than diagnostic
categories is obtained by considering the physical, mental and
social flexibility and adaptability of these children. In this regard,
their abilities were widely distributed. Six of the 14 children were
not toilet trained. Toilet training was an area of considerable

stress for the parents, not only because of the frustration and the
unpleasant task it routinely entailed, but because one criterion
for acceptance into the only public school facility in the area for
trainable retarded children was that the child be toilet trained.
(This was not an official criterion for acceptance as given by
state law. However, it was an acknowledged unofficial school
policy.) Most of the children were non-verbal. In fact only four of
the 14 children in this series had a limited but conversational use
of language. Four had "simple speech," i.e. used simple words or
sentence fragments. Six were non-verbal. A more complete consideration of indicators of social adaptability will follow with a
discussion of how the children were grouped within the Pre-
school.

THE PRE-SCHOOL PROGRAM

The Pre-school children were separated for more formal activities into three groups: the "Straight Line," the "Triangle" and
the "Circle" groups. The Pre-school director described these three
groups as follows:

> We divide the children into three groups. One we call the
> "Straight Line" group. These children can only learn, can
> only progress, through an intense one-to-one relationship. We
> often call this "eyeball-to-eyeball teaching." Our second
> group we call a "Triangle" group. These children are learn-
> ing what it means to be a part of a group. This group may be
> two children or up to four. It is a triangle because the learn-
> ing is through the teacher. The child learns to do his work or
> to keep his hands off the other child, not because of inner
> motivation, but because he likes and wants to please his
> teacher. The teacher is a focal point in this group and it is
> through her that the child learns to relate to other children
> and to work materials. The third group is the "Circle" group.
> These children can to some extent be a group with its mem-
> bers interacting and molding each other. The teacher may at
> times be in the center of the circle; she may be part of the
> circle; at times she may even be outside of the circle.

A description of these groups and their activities, as well as
the roles of teachers, parents and volunteers in the school pro-

gram, will be presented below. I will begin with the director's philosophy of education, since it was essentially upon this that the program was based. This outlook may be summarized by the following five points.

1. Every child was expected to try to learn.

2. Every child was expected to progress. Both the children and the staff were encouraged not to rest on their laurels. Positive change over time, while welcome, was not viewed as success but was seen as a new stage in the child's development from which to secure and extend this gain to a higher stage in his development.

3. Growth was seen not only in physical and intellectual terms but also in terms of social and emotional maturation. The child's growth was seen as a function of how well the school had succeeded in nurturing and integrating all four of these factors.

4. An attempt was made to teach a process of learning rather than some particular academic skill. The child was taught to master the steps necessary to complete the process of making a choice, doing work, cleaning up, and going on to another task. Once learned, this process was viewed as transferable to many different situations.

5. The staff attempted to establish and maintain a degree of flexibility between their line of control and the child's free choice. The younger the child, the more retarded the child, or the more disturbed the child, the less free choice. Greater degrees of freedom were extended when the child was able to handle the responsibility that freedom implies. In fact, one of the ultimate goals of the school as seen by the teachers was that of teaching the child to handle freedom.

The Pre-school was a cooperative venture organized around the director, a second teacher, a social worker, the parents, teacher aides, volunteers and the children themselves. Parents gave one school day a week to the Pre-school. Three parents were scheduled to be in attendance on any one day. They were under the supervision of the two teachers and served as teacher's aides. They assisted in watching the children and were responsible for preparing food during "juice time" (about 10:30), as well as the noon meal. While the school was run by the two teachers (one of whom was the directress), and a social worker, the parents had an active voice in helping to form school policy through their compulsory participation in an evening parent meeting that occurred on a once-a-month basis.

The ratio of students to teachers and helpers varied. As a rule, there was one teacher and teacher's aide to eight children. This did not include the supervised assistance of three parents who daily participated on a rotating basis. During the summer sessions, June 17 to July 26, the parents were not a part of the program. For this period of time, high school volunteers assumed the parents' duties. They too were supervised by the teachers.

The following is a description of the Pre-school program in terms of a "typical" day. The children usually arrived by 9:30 A.M. The program began with all three groups participating in "good morning time." During this period the children sat with the teachers, two aides, and three parents, (or student volunteers) on low benches arranged in a U-shaped configuration. The school's director sat at the front of the room with everyone facing her. Everyone participated in singing the "good morning song" that included each of the children's names. After this the director said good morning to each of the children individually. Upon hearing his name called, the child walked, ran, or jumped up to her, and shook her hand, hugged her, or leaped into her lap. Those who were verbal and so inclined said good morning in return. This activity took about 20 minutes and always occurred as the first order of business.

The children then split up into the three groups. Each group had a "work time." This term was used instead of "learning time" or "study time" for the following reasons. First, an attempt was made to instill in the children the importance of work, so that they would come to view themselves as "productive human beings." Secondly, the word "work" was used for the parents' sakes, i.e. to indicate to them that it was the school's aim to teach the children how to accomplish work in general, as opposed to some particular skill such as reading, writing, or arithmetic. These tasks might be included in "work time" but were subservient to teaching the children how to work in general. This in turn required teaching the children how to attend a task long enough to learn it, which was in part a function of teaching them how to interact appropriately in a group. A child's success in accomplishing this or that task was seen as a secondary teaching goal, which would follow when the children were taught how to voluntarily interact with each other and the teacher in an appropriate and "meaningful way." Succeeding in this, from the teacher's perspective, was not seen as a unique undertaking, requiring a set of specific techniques peculiar to mentally retarded children, but was viewed as much the same problem one would encounter in teaching any child. It was the position of the staff that the success or failure of these teaching techniques could serve as positive or negative models for teaching in general. The directress put it this way:

> The greatest lesson I think we are learning again and again is that we cannot teach and talk about retarded children without connecting up with all children; we cannot plan and talk about children without connecting up with their adult roles in society. One cannot run a classroom or a school, without connecting up with other classrooms and schools. Finally, we feel that what we are doing at the Pre-school can have meaning and can highlight the needs of all children, especially those today called 'exceptional,' 'culturally deprived,' or any other child who does not comfortably fit into the 'normal middle-class oriented school.'

This philosophy of education, i.e. that educational programs for the retarded should be seen in the broader context of educating children, is much more a part of educational programs for the retarded in other countries.[1] Such an outlook is in contradistinction to a movement in the United States toward greater "specialization" and "professionalization" in "special education."

The following is a description of some of the activities of these three groups and how they were designed to fit the educational philosophy previously outlined. I will begin by considering some of the activities common to all three groups.

"PAINTING TIME"

"Painting time" was a common activity. It was done at an easel with brush and poster paint, often "a la Pollack" or on a paper placed on a flat table top or the floor in the case of finger and/or toe painting. While painting was an individual undertaking, each child took a turn at it, and in this sense it was a group activity. As with all the program's activities, painting was designed to serve a special purpose. The teacher put it this way:

If and when a child learns to make the decision to finger paint, if he can choose the paints and put them on the paper himself, if he can make a picture which pleases him and put his picture on a rack, and then can clean up the table and wash his hands, he has accomplished a completion of a process. If he gets to this point he can then use the same process for many activities in his life—at home, at school, and anywhere else. This in no way means all our children can learn the total process before they are eight, but they can certainly be encouraged to do as much as possible.

Some of the paintings were cut and framed and constituted material for a yearly art show open to the public and presented at a University facility used to provide local professional and amateur artists with a forum throughout the year. The children's art was at this time placed on sale to the public. This provided a means of acquainting the public with the Pre-school, for the children to see their art displayed in public, for the children and parents to appear in public, a secondary way of raising funds for the school, and perhaps most important a means of consolidating the interests and energies of the parents in a common effort they all viewed as useful and important.

"DANCE TIME"

Another common activity of all three groups was "dance time." This block of time was considered an important part of the program. First, it served as a means of providing the children with a vehicle of individual expression and secondly it encouraged their free and spontaneous performance before others. In addition to offering a form of free expression, a part of dance time was used to develop discipline. Not all dance time was "free time." The children were taught to perform certain exercises such as crawling in a circle on their hands and knees, walking on their hands while the teacher held their legs up (wheelbarrow game), or crawling on their stomachs under low benches. All of these in time resulted in the child's developing his coordination, self-esteem and ability to perform successfully in public. For some this led to more formal dances and a situation in which all the children were able to perform as a group in a dance program. The dance program, as well as the art show, provided yet another means for the children and parents to appear in public, as well as providing both with a way of directing their interests and energies to the furtherance of an educational, rehabilitational, and therapeutic form of interaction.

"Play Time"

"Play Time" was the third common activity. When the weather permitted, this took place on a fenced playground adjacent to the school. There were no scheduled activities during this period. The only constraints upon the children were those that were binding within the school building, namely that one child does not hurt another. Some children rode or pushed tricycles, rode in or pulled others in a wagon, played in a sandbox, played with each other or went off to be by themselves. There was generally an effort made to discourage the children from going off by themselves. They were encouraged to play or at least interact together. Here it is difficult to generalize. Some children, depending upon their level of development, length of stay at the school, "bad day syndrome" or some other personal consideration, were left alone when alone. In another instance, a child was allowed to push another (if no harm came to the second) if this represented for the first a "coming out." One's self-esteem was seen to rely upon one's ability to influence one's environment, and one way to succeed in this was through the use of force, both in the form of action and/or reaction. Notwithstanding the fact that force was sometimes viewed as an adaptive technique, if the child resorting to it was much bigger, or prone to violence, etc., it was not allowed. In short, there was no standing rule for this or that form of behavior in the playground situation. Whether or not it was allowed or prevented depended for the most part upon the situation in which it occurred and the individual participants. Not everyone at the school was presumed competent to evaluate these complex sets of variables for a given situation. In order to "'meet the child at his own level", one had to be able to assess that level. Only the directress and other teacher were held to be competent in this regard. It was the teachers who were officially in charge. However, notwithstanding official policy and the parents' or volunteers' general orientation to the Pre-school's rules, there occurred in the everyday course of events situations in which subordinates had to evaluate a situation and act upon that assessment. The two teachers could not be present to mediate every encounter of the children with each other or with parents (or volunteers). This led to a wide range of variability in the adults' or teenagers' ways of coping with a given situation, especially on the playground. The school's staff was aware of this, and because consistency in handling situations was seen as a key factor in ultimately promoting acceptable forms of behavior in the children, the two teachers had certain reservations about leaving the children in the care of others, even though they recognized the necessity of doing so. This was seen as less of a problem within the school building itself since the teachers were present, in charge, and in a more structured situation. The children were within easy reach and, unlike the playground situation, appropriate interventions were more likely to be effectively initiated. In light of the above, it is perhaps not surprising to find that the teachers were usually a little apprehensive about activities that were out of their direct view or control.

"Work Time"

Apart from common activity time, the three groups of children had specific and separate tasks for "work time." For example, the "Straight Line" children worked with "dough." Dough was the consistency of clay, was prepared by the teacher, came in a variety of colors and was harmless if swallowed. The children kneaded it, rolled it out with rollers, squeezed it between their fingers, cut it into shapes with cookie cutters and not infrequently ate it. Apart from working with dough, they piled large cardboard blocks, played on a small slide or with a sturdy wooden car large enough to sit in, threw balls or caught bean bags. All play materials were simple, sturdy, safe, well-worn and few in number. The staff or volunteers also worked with the children individually during this period in an attempt to get them to recognize objects of different sizes and colors. In this regard the most popular game was that of putting different colored rings in descending diameters on a stick.

The more advanced children participated in tasks more often associated with a formal education. However, these tasks too were always viewed within the context of what was necessary for an education in general. The teacher in charge of "work time" for the "Triangle" and "Circle" groups put it this way:

> . . . There are certain basic things which all small children need to learn, whether they begin learning them at age four or whether they begin learning them at age eight . . . there are still basic things all small children do. They have to learn to relate to one another within a group, they have to learn to cope with a school situation of some kind and then they have to learn to match two items which are the same, find out what is different, learn colors, counting if they are up to it, while they are still here.

The following is a description of selected "work time" activities of the "Triangle" and "Circle" groups and their implications for the teacher and child as seen from the teacher's perspective:

> It's hard for me to talk in large generalizations. I keep going back to one . . . you say puzzles. O.K., take puzzles. Um, the essential thing behind puzzles, what manufacturers think they are doing is, ah . . . a good deal of small muscle manipulation, I think that's what it is and visual perception, putting something together as a whole. Anyway the way our school is set up, that's nice. It's nice to have the kids learn to use their fingers properly and it's nice that they begin to see bits and pieces as a whole. But there's an awful lot going on when there's a group of kids, just four children doing puzzles. Every one of those kids is getting something dif-

ferent out of doing that puzzle. . . . I may have a child sitting next to me who's really pretty scattered. And that child is terrified all the time that he's doing that puzzle because it's broken. And will be panicked about puzzles and will have a hard time even taking it out, for if he takes it out then he's killed it. And that will frighten him so terribly that it'll take all of our energy to get that puzzle put back together. That's one thing that he's doing. I've got another one off in the corner who can do a puzzle, now. No sweat. No problem. He can put it together. He's licked all the little problems like that. So the only thing he's doing now is either pleasing me or not pleasing me or getting my attention. So he's not going to put that puzzle together that day. Maybe he'll sit and bank pieces or drop them on the floor or put them in his pocket or hide them somewhere or throw them out the window. And another child really enjoys putting puzzles together because he related better to things than he does to anyone else. And he gets down behind that puzzle and he'll put puzzles together all day long because it's the safest thing to do. And there will be maybe another child who's eager to please, who's been patterned to do what the authority figures ask because then he's a good boy, he's good. I did it, see I did it, it's good. And if you asked him what he put together, he wouldn't be able to tell you. He just put it together and gave it to you and said—look, good. Now I'm all right. So that's a lot the way things work.

. . . So that most things that I do, whether it's matching flannel board pieces or, um, basic counting, putting a Montessori form thing together or those little Dutch puzzles with the graduated sizes for fruit, putting animals together, drawing, whatever it is that we do, that's a device to do—to get the kids going, to get them doing something which is constructive and which is structured. So that they can find out that they can do something. . . . I can take one single activity —I have some great big alphabet cards which I have never used as alphabet cards. I'm just starting to now. They're large, simple, whole word pictures of easily recognizable objects; cats and dogs and birds and oranges and flowers and so on and houses. With that . . . first group of mine . . . we would just name those items and I figured I can use this because all of them need practice in talking and two of them need practice in or need more experience; they need a broader life experience. They cannot always recognize that a house is a house is a house, whether it's a two-story or made out of brick or white with green shutters. Um, so once they recognize all the objects, then I start laying them down on the table, a whole bunch of them, instead of me just holding them up—what's this, and putting it down and what's this, your turn, go on—um, and I would say then, O.K., Jimmy, find me the house. And he would find the house. Then we moved on to a point where they knew the things so well that we could say—I could have among other things, a people house and a tree, you know, a house people live in—only people live in houses, and then a tree and then I could say, someone give me a bird. O.K. Now—can you find me a place where birds live? And he could give me the tree. And then—can you find me the place where people live? And so from just holding things up and naming them, it becomes quite complicated. And then when they've gotten all the little clues down, then I let them be the teacher. They can take a turn asking someone for something in the same way.

. . . This is where I'm always trying to get to that place where a child can communicate well enough and be confident enough to take over this much and be teacher. Because it's always when I've gotten to that point, where the kid can be teacher for a while, that we've been the most successful. . . . I find out all sorts of interesting things then—about the children and about what I taught them and whether it's been useful or not, because the children are very selective and very careful and at that point toss out everything that wasn't useful to them and concentrate only on what was useful. And it's a lesson; you can really be surprised the first time you do it. . . .

THE RETARDED AS TEACHERS

These closing remarks by the teacher on "work time" leads the author to a consideration of why the prospect of a retarded child serving as teacher need not be viewed as an instance of his "playing teacher," or when it is taken seriously, not seen as a case of "the blind leading the blind." Not only may retarded children teach other retarded children, but they may teach normal children

or the teacher. The following are some examples of this taken
from the transcribed verbatim accounts of teachers. One teacher
of retarded children (I.Q.'s 30-52) at a state residence center
gave this account:

> Tommie . . . learned it so he could be teacher (holding up
> cards and getting the children to answer appropriately). And
> he would go around and make the kids go through their
> paces, in the right hand, left hand activity. He can do a lot
> of the language things. And he's meaner than the teacher—
> well, you've got to say it exactly right, or he won't let you
> off the hook. And he can keep control over the whole group
> except Janie and Nick. Those kids don't get up out of their
> chairs when Tommie's up there teaching. Boy, they just
> better sit or they're going to get cracked on the noggin or
> something. I don't know what he's got on them. But the
> kids have a natural desire to want to do this, but they have
> to be taught to do it well. They have to be taught to carry
> through. . . . Tommie has to be taught how to be a good
> teacher, and then he will be. He has a natural ability to do
> it. And a natural desire to do it.

Another teacher of "educable" retarded children in an integrated public school (a school accommodating retarded and normal
children) had this to say about a program she helped initiate,
where retarded children taught normal children:

> So one of the best things that we did, it sustained itself
> over those seven years, there happened to be a nursery
> school right on the grounds and at that time the director
> of it was a woman, her name was Mrs. H., . . . I had never
> met the woman before but I one day spoke to my fellow
> teacher and said, "I think this is a good place for our chil-
> dren to work." And he said, "what can they do?" He had
> never been in a nursery school. So I said, "they can do many
> things. They can help the cooks, they can work with young
> children." And so we sent a note to Mrs. H. asking her if
> we could come and talk to her about something that would
> be mutually advantageous. . . . And Mrs. H. was amused
> at these off-beat upstarts who were questioning what they
> could do with retarded youngsters. In the meanwhile, we

went to the curriculum head and—so that we wouldn't get into difficulty—and indicated to him that we thought that this was something that could be good. The man was and is a very fine person. And he was . . . he became interested in what we were attempting and he gave us a lot of support. And, uh, he was willing to come with us to discuss what it was that retarded youngsters could do with normal children in a child care center. . . . We outlined something that we would experiment with. And this was that we would bring out children—incidentally, the only thing that we specified in anything that we did was that all the children must try everything. . . . And we learned that doors were closed and this is something to remember; certainly this is true about us as individuals—how many times am I afraid to try something and I won't? . . . And Mrs. H. was very willing to accept this (that we all try), she said sure.

So then how does it work out? For the last seven years twice a week either Mr. T. takes a group of seven or eight students and then another day I take a group of seven or eight students. His surplus students I take care of when he goes there (to the nursery school); my surplus he takes care of. In other words, we don't flood the normal with the retarded; we try to be a little bit, uh, uh, what shall I say . . . subtle about it. . . . I would say that some of the best things that happened to our children happened in the nursery school, not in our classroom. They learned to develop and they learned to use skills. The children will sometimes read to the other kids. But they are motivated into reading because children are very interested in stories. Or if they can't read, they pretend to read (to the normal nursery school children). And this is just as good. This is probably a step toward reading. There is conversation. They find that very young children will listen to them. Whereas their contemporaries, normal contemporaries, might get very impatient. They found that their bizarre behavior at times, especially when we have a very disturbed youngster, and we have had the most schizoid of them all, does not offend young children. Young children are very accepting of anything. . . . The only people who are bothered and who are bothered from time to time are the adults, the teachers, not the children. They are completely accepting.

The following are some of the ways in which retarded children succeeded in teaching the teacher. One such way was previously noted in the account of the Pre-school teacher on page 55. This can be described as follows. The teacher was able to see what information the child had retained, (what from her perspective she believed the child considered most helpful), from what the child in the role of teacher presented to her in class. By remembering what she had previously offered the child, she could see what he did not retain, i.e. what she presumed he did not consider helpful. She could then reevaluate the nature of the material she would offer him in the future. In short, she tried to give the child future information that he had told her (by his teaching) he would be able to assimilate. The teacher, because of her belief that the child had selected to retain from her prior offerings that which was helpful to him, felt that by maximizing and perpetuating this process she was being most helpful. The net result of this was that the child was teaching the teacher what it was he wanted her to teach him, at the same time that the teacher believed that she had selected to teach the child those things she felt would be most helpful. Not only did she believe that she was being helpful, but because she felt the child was happy with the help she had given him, she was happy. Once established, this process was self-perpetuating.

The author includes a discussion of this point not in order to argue the merits of the case. The child may or may not have benefitted most by the teacher adopting the set of assumptions noted above and acting on them the way she did. The point is that the teacher was not aware of the process that she had both initiated and was subject to, and was unable therefore to assess the merits of it for herself. It was to bring this particular instance of the general case of "the teacher learning from her pupils" into focus that the above analysis was offered.

Another instance of the teacher learning from her pupils was offered by a teacher of "educable" retarded children. Because this account was related to the author at the very end of the interview and after the tape on the tape recorder had run out, I can only offer the gist of it to the reader. The teacher, it seems, at some indefinite point in her teaching career (she had taught retarded children for 11 years), decided it might be amusing and/or instructive to let one or another of her better pupils "play teacher." Periodically, as the fancy took her, she would select a candidate to "play teacher." Before long, she found to her chagrin that the child refused to "'play teacher" but would gladly play *the* teacher. In doing so he or she portrayed, for the class, a caricature of the teacher teaching. If the teacher was in the habit of scratching her head, the child scratched his head. More unseemly habits of the teacher were also imitated and expanded upon. The teacher, upon receiving the power "to see herself as others saw her" (a latent function of the child playing *the* teacher that she felt was better left latent), in time discontinued this practice, but not without acknowledging to the author how instructive and distressing it had been for her.

PROJECTED EDUCATIONAL CAREERS

I have outlined some of the games, tasks, and playthings, that constituted the activities of the "Straight Line," "Triangle" and "Circle" children at the Pre-school. What is left out of these accounts, of course, are the kinds of interactions that developed over time between the children and teachers, and the children themselves. These can best be summarized as tending to move from "inappropiate to appropriate," from "egoistic" to "social" and from immoral or amoral to moral. The extent to which this process succeeded was, from the perspective of the lay public, greater among the "Triangle" and "Circle" children. While children in any one of these three categories might pass from one into any of the others, the "Straight Line" children were least likely to do so. More often than not these children, because they could not get into the public facilities for "trainable" children upon leaving pre-school, (and there were no other alternatives available to the parent), were either kept at home or ultimately institutionalized. Those in the other two groups usually went from the Pre-school at age eight into a "trainable" facility where they remained until they were 18. Some children, usually from the "Circle" group, went into "educable classes" for the retarded or special classes for the "educationally handicapped" within the regular public school system. The latter usually had a higher I.Q. than the others but were unable to perform up to their potential because of emotional problems.

A follow-up study of the careers of children in the author's series who left the Pre-school, revealed that since the time of the first interview, a total of six children had left the Pre-school program. Four of these left as a result of the age limit, i.e. they had reached the age of eight. Two left before reaching the age limit. One, a boy, moved to another city. At last report, the parents were trying hard to find this child a suitable educational program. The other child, a girl, who left the program before reaching the age limit, had only been at the Pre-school for a period of six months before being placed in a private school for the retarded. This occurred as a result of the unexpected availability of a subsidy, since the expense of a private facility would have been prohibitive for all of the families in this series. Of the remaining four children, two are currently enrolled in a school for "trainable" retarded children, while the other two, unable to enter the program for trainable children, are currently awaiting institutionalization.

PARENTAL EVALUATIONS OF THE PRE-SCHOOL PROGRAM

Notwithstanding the public's tendency to see tangible progress only among the "Circle" and "Triangle" children, the parents and teachers saw it taking place in all three groups. Parents from each group of children, from the least to the most promising, felt their children had benefitted from the Pre-school program. It was typical of the parents in all three groups that they were optimistic that their child would at least get into the facility for trainable children upon leaving he Pre-school.

Why were the parents from the most to the least promising groups of children equally optimistic? The answer to this has been dealt with at least in part in Chapter I. However, there were other factors involved. The parents' compulsory participation in the Pre-school activities insured their acquaintance with other retarded children of a wide range of potentialities. The parents also discussed informally among themselves the practical problems of child management as well as their domestic life. As a result of these interactions and their therapeutic influence, and through a process not fully grasped by the author, the mothers of the most and the least promising children spontaneously offered statements the gist of which was: "it could be worse." In short, every mother interviewed felt that her child was better off than many others at the Pre-school—lay opinions and professional evaluations to the contrary notwithstanding. A mother of a child in the "Straight Line" group had this to say:

> I really do (think she would enjoy working with retarded children) . . . you know, when you live with one child at home, it's different. You know you say to yourself—gee, how am I going to like it being around 15 other kids (as they are required to do at the Pre-school); They're not all going to be my sweet little Johnnie. But when I was here 10 minutes, I realized how much luckier I was than some of the other parents.

Another parent, whose child was in the "Circle" group, gave this account:

> We see evidence now, of several things that she does now, indicate that she just wasn't ready or she was in the wrong environment around children who she knew were not her peers at the time (in a regular public school). They were just too much for her. She just couldn't cope with them. And these children (at the Pre-school) they're children with problems a little more severe than hers, which gives her an opportunity to be the leader and not the follower. Which is helping her quite a bit.

A ready answer frequently invoked by evaluation teams for why parents tend to view their children's potential "unrealistically" is based upon the notion of an unconscious automatic defensive repression of the all-too-painful truth. The author feels that a more consistent and parsimonious explanation of this phenomenon than one based on Freud's "unconscious" is found in Sartre's notion of "self-deception" or "bad faith."

Bad faith or self-deception is the act of lying to oneself. A person is aware of the truth but tries to hide it from himself. He is the deceiver and the deceived simultaneously and knows that he has deceived himself. He believes the lie he has created and hides from himself the fact that he is the creator of the falsehood. He is fleeing from the truth, but he is not totally unaware that he is fleeing. . . . There are two levels of awareness; one is simple (like the pre-reflective consciousness), the other involves attending or noticing (like the reflective consciousness). In this way I can be aware of something without at the same time attending to it. . . . Self-deception is possible because a person may yield to one belief by lying to himself and by failing to notice or by ignoring the truth of the matter. In addition to being logically possible, this account conforms to the way in which people talk of such matters in ordinary language. Thus they would say of the mother who has come to believe that her son is a fine fellow, that she knows all along IN SOME CORNER OF HER MIND that he is not much good.[2]

Apart from the way in which parents at the Pre-school tended to evaluate the status and potential of their children was the way in which they evaluated the influence of the program upon themselves.

Mother: I think probably the most helpful person was Mrs. H. (the directress). She has a tremendous understanding of children. Of course, she's not working necessarily with re-tarded children (some were emotionally disturbed, brain-damaged, etc.). She had a very calming effect in that she was able to read so much about him and see the positive things. Things I was maybe too emotionally bundled up in to see myself. But there were other people who would talk in circles (other professionals) and this was very disturbing . . . to us I think.

Int.: Who do you talk to (about her problems)?

Mother: Who do I talk to?

Int.: Still the physician?

Mother: No. I probably come here and say something to the teachers here. Try to find something out that way. But it's difficult because no one has answers. But even though you know no one has answers, you need someone looking at you very calmly and saying, well, this is a plateau; I've seen this happen before, or something. . . .

Int.: If arrangements were different and you didn't have to do this (give time at the Pre-school), do you think you would still. . . .

Mother: Well, in some ways I would feel, well, then I would be losing contact. You know, because coming here you see the other children and you're watching your own child with them, and I can see what's happening. But when I'm away I can't. I think this is a good thing to do.

One mother had this to say:

But I think that, ah,—these things (the education of parents), they should break the parents down into small groups and really and truly educate them. Because . . . this . . . I've really been more enlightened about the whole situation in the short time I've been coming out here (to the Pre-school). I don't know whether it's because I've seen the other children, or what it is.

Another put it this way:

I feel he's going the right way, yes. Because I mean, here, just last year, see, Bruce was one of the activist kids here at the school and he was climbing and jumping, just going everywhere, and it was hard for the teacher to keep up with him. And the teacher says that Bruce has slowed down and he's paying more attention. When you hear a report like that, you've got to feel yourself that he is coming around in the right step. And that's what I feel I'd like for my doctor to say.

Thus far in the chapter, I have discussed how the parents and children started upon their educational careers, the characteristics of the Pre-school parents and children, a description of the Pre-school's educational program, the role of the retarded child as teacher, and finally the parents' evaluation of the program for their children and themselves. This brings me to a discussion of the nature of facilities generally available for the retarded, the role of administrators, the qualifications of the teachers, and how all of these factors affect the prospects of establishing a program of mass education for the retarded. I will begin this discussion by contrasting some of the perspectives and practices of mass education for normal children with those of the retarded.

THE EDUCATION OF NORMAL CHILDREN

The public education of normal children has generally proceeded according to certain theoretical perspectives about the nature of the child and how he can best learn and benefit in later life from the methods of education he was subject to in his youth. These perspectives have, in the last fifty years or so, shifted from rote learning en masse, learning of ABC's and multiplication tables, to learning through doing, the whole word method of reading, and the "new math."

Theoretical justification has always accompanied these shifts in educational perspectives and practices, notwithstanding the fact that there is little empirical evidence to indicate the superiority of one teaching perspective or practice over another.[3] In spite of this, it was common for claims of superiority to be made which ultimately resulted in the implementation of programs. No matter which program was in vogue and for whatever reason, the need was felt to standardize teaching procedures in order to expedite the coming of mass education.

Teachers are initiated into the standardization of practices during their student careers. The teaching techniques considered to be best suited for the purpose of achieving the then prevalent goals of education are incorporated into the teacher's curriculum. The prospective teachers are then graded on a number of criteria, one of which is the degree of their adherence to these procedures during the student teacher training period. This is followed by an on-the-job evaluation where the teacher is expected to continue to adhere to standard operating procedures. In addition to this, the State generally issues the books to be used at the various levels, as well as other constraints that further work to insure a measure of standardization.

Such attempts to standardize curriculums and goals, of course, recognize that even under the most favorable conditions, individual differences exist within the group. Some children have a greater intellectual potential, motivation, or predisposition towards learning than others. However, it is assumed that within limits a curriculum can be expected to succeed reasonably well with the entire group, notwithstanding individual variation in performance.[4] In short, it is generally held that normal children, properly "screened," will be able to adapt to both the goals and standard operating procedures of public education and benefit, to one extent or another, from this experience.

Granting that teachers only imperfectly adhere to the rules and methods of teaching (as it was taught to them), and that the nature of educational programs varies between states, school districts or even classrooms, it is also true that things are sufficiently the same to provide for the "rational" production of the large number of teachers necessary to carry on a program of mass education for millions of normal school age children. Nor are programs and teachers so different that the tremendous residential mobility of the American public does not allow for a relatively easy transition for both teachers and children when moving from state to state, school to school or classroom to classroom. Finally, a given of the mass education of normal children is that it is compulsory.

TEACHING THE RETARDED: "PLAYING IT BY EAR"

Such are some of the general practices, assumptions and expectations of mass education for normal children. This perspective is conspicuously absent, however, in the case of teaching the retarded. There is no consensus here on either the goals or practices of education, nor from the teacher's point of view is there currently a training program that actually prepares the teacher for teaching.[5] In brief, notwithstanding the efforts or contentions of administrators in the field of special education, the prospect of standardizing goals, teaching practices, or teaching curriculums for the retarded is neither to be found nor anticipated in the foreseeable future.

The question arises as to why this situation exists, when it is estimated that there are currently six million retarded children and adults in the country.[6] At least 85% of these are "mildly retarded,"[7] i.e. I.Q. 55-69, or within the "educable" range. Most of the remaining 15% are "trainable." In short, only a very few of the retarded would be unable to benefit from some form of educational program. It would seem, under the circumstances, that the need for a program of mass education is clearly indicated. This is especially true when we allow that the major objections to the mass education of normal children have for the most part long since been silenced. Some of these were that children are individuals with different temperaments, personalities, I.Q.'s, social skills, etc. As much can be said for the retarded. I.Q. spans in normal classes are likely to fall within a range differential of twenty points. I.Q.'s among "trainable" or "educable" retarded children in California classrooms are also within this order of difference. There are differences in cultural and class background among normal children. This is true as well among the retarded. Normal children have distinct personality differences and exhibit a wide range of social skills. This is also true among the retarded.

Why then has there been an effort to standardize the practices and goals of public education among normal children in the name of greater efficiency and the achievement of mass education, while the practices and goals of teaching the retarded are still subject to the inclinations of the particular teacher? Standard operating procedure for the teachers of the retarded is to "play it by ear." As a general rule, they proceed according to the following formula: "it's good if it works." The consensus among the teachers studied was that there is no particular way to proceed, and any or all of the different means used by different teachers are equally good if they "work."[8]

Education in this setting is viewed as tailormade to meet the individual at "his own level." The desire, on the part of the teachers, to achieve this form of student-teacher interaction is in

the best teaching tradition. The questions that usually go un-
answered or unasked are how one assesses the child's "own level"
and how it is possible to deal with the children on a one-to-one
basis given the number of retarded who are "trainable," "educable," or otherwise require some form of education, and the number of teachers of the retarded available for the task.

> . . . many states even now do not provide any classes for
> the 'trainable' retarded, and no state has enough classes for
> the 'educable' retarded. Only one of every five retarded
> children is now being reached by any kind of special educa-
> tion program. The President's Panel found 20,000 special
> education teachers across the nation, many of them poorly
> trained, where 55,000 were needed. The Panel predicted that
> by 1970 the need for special teachers will reach 90,000.[9]

Another aspect rarely dealt with is what is meant by "if it
works." What is it that happens when "something works"? The
individual teachers interviewed by the author had in mind a wide
range of goals. Yet each teacher seems to have felt that all
teachers were seeking the same goals (undefined) and that whatever succeeded in achieving them (the means were also extremely
ambiguous) was good. Whatever did not "work" was either bad
or in need of revision. It cannot be argued here that the above is
only the imperfect state of current affairs, and that the teachers
themselves felt that a standardization of teaching methods and/or
goals was either possible or desirable. The fact is they did not.
How then will a relatively small group of teachers of the retarded
in public schools, clinics, state institutions and private schools
succeed in educating six million retarded children and adults?

The lack of standardization of teaching methods and goals is
particularly telling on the retarded. Retarded children are shifted
from school to school when facilities are available. When they are
not, they are institutionalized or kept at home. Only about half
of San Francisco's "trainable" children are receiving any sort of
public education.[10] In San Francisco, the Pre-school previously
described enrolls about 14 children between the ages of four to
eight. From there some of those at the "trainable" level will be
able to go on to the public facility for "trainable" children ages

eight to 18. It is different from the Pre-school in both goals and methods. Some Pre-school children go on to "educable" classes. These too are different from the Pre-school in orientation and also vary considerably from one school district to another, and even from class to class within the same school. For example, some of these are integrated into normal school facilities on the "educable" level; others are not. On the "trainable" level, none are. When public facilities are not available, as is not infrequently the case for "trainable" retarded children, those parents able to afford it may place their child in a private school. These too are very often different from the public facilities in both teaching techniques and ultimate teaching goals and, of course, they vary widely among themselves.

Others have indicated the debilitating effect of a discontinuous school career upon normal children, resulting from the sudden loss of meaningful social relationships.[11] This is especially true for the retarded, not only because they are subject to many school changes, but because the schooling itself is so different from place to place, even within the same city, due to the lack of standardization of curriculums, outlooks or even general orientations. Add to this the fact that the retarded child has a harder time adjusting to his environment, and one can readily see the detrimental effects of an inconsistent and discontinuous educational career, not only upon learning, but also upon the development of the retarded child's level of social adaptability. One pre-school parent expressed her concern this way:

She's (the retarded child) asserting herself a lot more. When she started talking to people, I would have to say to her: 'say hello,' or 'say this,' or 'say goodbye,' and when she went to say it, she would whisper. You would never hear what she said. So now I still sometimes have to tell her, and I will also say, 'say it so you can be heard.' And she shouts it out. She's coming right out with it. So I don't know. I think too that, I think about this sometimes. If she were taken out of this environment (the Pre-school) and placed in another with completely different people, what would be her feeling then? If she were maybe transferred to another school when it comes time to leave here, this bothers me a lot too. I think about it. . . . And I'm anxious about that. If she can adjust when it comes time to leave here, then I feel she has accomplished an awful lot. Because this is kind of home to her now. This is her second home. And if she can be taken from one situation and placed in another and still get along the way she gets along now, I will feel that she has made tremendous progress. And I keep wondering if that's going to be the case.

The above conditions also pose certain key questions for educators: 1) how would one evaluate the relative success or failure of a teaching program if each teacher proceeded according to his own inclinations and these inclinations remained ill-defined or unknown? 2) how would one initiate change in teaching methods, goals or expectations under these conditions? and 3) given the above, how would one go about achieving greater control of these situations so as to be able to achieve No. 1 and No. 2 without putting teacher incentive or creativity in jeopardy? These problems are not unique to educational programs. They are characteristic of formal organizations in general.[12] As such, they have been recognized, if not entirely solved, in the pursuit of mass education for normal children, but have thus far received little serious consideration by the teachers or administrators of educational programs for the retarded.

This oversight on the part of both teachers and administrators, it may be argued, stems from the fact that many of the teachers interviewed by the author had begun teaching the retarded when little in the way of special education was required, and little was being done to develop or implement a plan or even guidelines for the mass education of the retarded. However, others had begun teaching more recently, i.e. within the last few years, and it was their opinion that things had not changed appreciably. Also, many of the former, while they began to teach without special training, had since taken special education courses. The problem was not a lack of orientation but rather one of faulty orientation. There was a general agreement among all the teachers that their special training had proved to be of little or no assistance in the classroom.

It is true that there are now many more college classes and curriculums designed to meet the needs of special education. It is probably true also that the administrators responsible for establishing and implementing these programs feel they are meeting a need. However, from the teachers' perspective, these programs were ill-conceived. Teachers subject to this special training found themselves quickly disenchanted when they sought to put the goals and practices of these programs into operation. The problem of rectifying these shortcomings was compounded by the fact that the student teachers were reluctant to advise the instructor of the course's shortcomings during the training period. After the fact, when the student became a licensed teacher and was actually employed in the classroom, the instructor was no longer available and feedback was impossible. At that point, with respect to their employer, acknowledgment that their prior training had been inadequate or inapplicable would, in effect, be an admission of incompetence, or at the very least, that they lacked the special competence their training implied. Consequently, the teachers were unable to implement the standardization of practices and goals given by their "special education," not only because of their inappropriateness, but because the teachers were unable to effect the means of making them more appropriate.

The inability of the teacher to help revise some of these faulty assumptions was a function of more than a problem in communication. This was only one contributing factor. It was also affected by the power of the administrator over the teacher and the latter's inability to influence policy even when he tried to. This aspect will be discussed in greater detail later in the chapter under a discussion of the teacher's role (or lack of it) in contributing to curriculums and state guidelines.

While it is true that the programs for the retarded envisioned by the administrators of special education courses were not being implemented, those authorized and responsible for presenting these methods and goals to the student teacher in the name of trying to establish a better public education program for the retarded seemed to feel they were being implemented. The net result in terms of teacher practices was the perpetuation of "playing it by ear" and the institutionalization of arbitrary "it's good if it works" procedures.

The Role of Administrators

Not all administrators of programs for the retarded were guilty of retarding the coming of mass education through a lack of communication or misunderstanding. Some sought to do so intentionally. For example, when integrated classes were first initiated in the San Francisco area, not all administrators were enthusiastic about implementing the program. One teacher gave this account:

> Some of the people who were supposed to know, like education professors, felt that retarded children really shouldn't be separated or isolated and that there were many things that they could get from associating with normal kids. This was generally accepted, you know, there is a whole concept in education about education for all children. And everybody is filled with that sort of thing. I mean particularly administrators here at least pay lip service to the idea, that the job of a public education system is to provide education for everybody. And so there's a lot of talk about doing this, but then I noticed that there wasn't too much enthusiasm about having retarded kids in the school, particularly in an upper middle class, upwardly mobile group of people in a bedroom community with kids all striving to go to college. The school was very much interested in academics and making good records and that kind of thing. And the teachers didn't really know too much about retarded children. I mean if you said retarded, they (and these teachers had a lot of teaching experience) would confuse the term retarded with crazy. I mean it's unbelievable but it's true. This was between 1956 and 1959.

Another, when asked about how the school program came to initiate integrated classes for the retarded, had this to say:

> Well, a lot of these programs grew up, you might say somewhat like Topsy, I mean they just grew up. Actually they didn't fit in very well—they had no building funds, and they

put them in a class wherever they could find a place to put them and then gradually as funds became available, things improved. At first many districts didn't or couldn't be bothered—by law if a district didn't have the retarded identified, they didn't need any (integrated) classes. Districts got by this little issue by not identifying them. And this district did somewhat the same, I mean progressed on somewhat the same basis.

Another administrative practice with respect to "identifying" the retarded was related to the author during a lecture by the head of special education classes at a state college. Here the question of "identification" was based upon economic considerations. Since the state paid public school facilities $375 per year per person enrolled in an "educable" program and $975 per annum per child in a "trainable" program, administrators tended to view questionable (and sometimes not so questionable) cases of retardation as "trainable." The above combined practices resulted in the "identification" of fewer "retarded" at one point in time and at another in the "identification" of larger numbers of "trainable" children than actually existed. The influence of these practices upon the rates of retardation, and the planning of programs based upon a consideration of these rates, is difficult to estimate. One thing is certain, and that is that an accurate assessment of the needs of the retarded was impossible, given these practices and others to be discussed later in the chapter. All of this, of course, says nothing of the consequences of these practices for children who were at one time or another deprived of an educational program or placed in one that was inappropriate.

One teacher's opinion of his principal's concern for initiating a curriculum best suited to the educational needs of the retarded in a then newly established integrated setting is as follows:

. . . and I was new, and you know, I was concerned with the school. I had gotten the impression that I could do whatever I wanted with these kids as long as I didn't make any waves; as long as I kept every one quiet and as long as I kept everyone busy.

The above statements deal with the period when integrated classes were first being established in the San Francisco area about ten years ago. One might expect that things have changed appreciably since then and that there is now an active concern for how and what the retarded are being taught. Another teacher, a doctoral candidate in education, had this to say about the current state of affairs:

> I think in many schools, I would say in most schools, they do not care what goes on in special education classes, as long as they don't make waves. And as long as these kids don't get sent to the office too often. If the class causes the administrators no problems, they can do most anything. I honestly believe that I could sit here with my kids all day and we could either watch television or we could listen to the radio or we could sit on the floor and play jacks all day long, every day, and I don't think anybody would care, as long as we didn't make too much noise. I really don't think they could care.

Apart from the general lack of communication between the teacher and administrator and the behind-the-scenes machinations of individual administrators of school districts, there is the question of teacher preparedness and the attitudes of the teachers themselves, as these relate to any effort to establish some meaningful programs of mass education for the retarded.

Teacher Preparedness and "Special Education"

Perhaps the best way to present the attitudes of the teachers towards teacher preparedness in general and the adequacy of "special education" in particular is to offer what they themselves had to say about it. One teacher had this to say about the state of her readiness to teach the retarded when she first began teaching ten years ago:

> The children just needed to be treated at their age level. And I was conducting a nursery school program. But at the same time I saw immediately it wasn't working. There was a child who was completely out in his own world—and there

was no equipment, and I had to makeshift all kinds of things. I wasn't talking to those children at all. One was obviously so severely retarded that he didn't belong there at all. There was really a terrible gap and they were unscreened completely. . . . It was really very extreme. Whoever fell into the category, whoever couldn't make it in the regular classroom, ended up here. I had a schizophrenic child among them. You know, it was very wild. And I said, this is impossible. I don't know what I'm doing and I have no frame of reference— although I was already taking a special course, but there had been absolutely nothing (relevant to this).

Another, who had just finished describing the circumstances under which she came to teach the retarded, went on to say:

So that's how I got here and I feel that it's my area of concentration. And I just love it. And I repeat again, because so many people have difficulty in believing me, I find a great joy in being with these kids and what they have to offer me in terms of how they are and how they behave. But it's been very difficult and I've certainly changed a great deal of my feelings about them as I've taught them, and a lot of the philosophies of education that I came out of college with that were so firm. When I first started to teach—it was the more severely retarded children. I had never worked with them. And at that time, these kids who came to school had never been to school. So it was an unknown situation to them. And my feeling then was that I wanted to be as free in the classroom and as unstructured as I could get away with. And it was pretty chaotic. I learned a tremendous amount and I still feel that some of my most creative teaching happened then. A lot of things happened, and I had so few preconceived ideas because I had no training in the field at all. I had never been with a retarded child except seeing that one group from a distance for five minutes. I had no idea how to teach them.

A third teacher gave this account:

And so I took a job and spent two years in teaching and counseling retarded children at a secondary level which means junior and senior high school level. These kids prob-

ably ranged between 14 and 18 years of age. And these were
an interesting group of kids, cause my first impression of
these kids was that they were totally and completely un-
responsive. I can remember the first day I went in there.
I had lesson plans. I had figured out what I was going to
teach them and what was important. I remember sitting
around in a group and sort of explaining and planning what
we were going to be doing and why we were going to be
doing that. I set it up in sort of a give and take kind of way,
almost a group discussion kind of thing because I wanted to
get some ideas from them about what was important to learn
and what we ought to do. And it was fantastic, you know,
like I set up some questions, or some ideas that I thought
would get some kind of interaction between the kids and me.
And you know, nothing happened at all. I mean they'd sit
there and look at me like I was, oh I don't know, so I tried
that, but not for too long. Also these kids had problems
too, you know, like they were difficult to manage, difficult
management problems.

What of those teachers one would assume were better prepared
to teach the retarded as a result of their courses in special education? The following is an account of one teacher (holder of a
Doctorate in Education) who had this to say about special education courses and curriculums designed to prepare the teacher for
the task of teaching the retarded:

But really, the classes that I've taken in special education
were farces as far as I'm concerned. And I probably
shouldn't say that, but if you want a true answer I have to.
I think it's a deplorable state of affairs—and this does not
pertain to special education specifically, it pertains in part
to the state credentialing set-up and also has something to
do with the training program for colleges. Because some of
these so-called 'special education' courses—you know, everyone has to take them. So they get through them the best way
they can. And I lived through that. They were worse than a
waste of time. They insulted my intelligence. That's really
the way I felt about it because—I couldn't take anything that
was related to what I needed. It had to be a course number
and, as I say, part of it was due to the lackadaisical attitude

of whoever had the class. . . . I found out then that a teacher
in the school who had taught the course had to take it herself,
I presume from someone else, in order to get a credential
for herself. Well, she had been teaching that course at a
college level for six or seven years. I mean this is not all
special education . . . this is part of the profession of teaching
and, of course, the California Teachers Association is working on it. . . . It's kind of a standing joke in California that
Toynbee couldn't teach a beginning history class in high
school and Einstein couldn't have taught a beginning high
school physics class.

Another teacher (the Doctoral candidate previously referred
to) put it this way:

. . . I wonder, maybe most of what I know that is . . . that
I feel is of value to the kids, if I hadn't just learned it on my
own, through trial and error. The courses I had at college
(in special education)—I'm not saying they did not have
value, because they did, but—I don't see how they really
helped me in the classroom. . . . Much of it has been unrealistic I feel. And I feel I'm a better judge of that than
the people who are throwing it at me because I actually
work with the retarded and they do not, and have not probably ever worked with them. And so I feel very often the
courses I'd had were not only not helpful, but actually they
were wrong. It gives you false impressions. You get the sort
of thing that just won't work in the classroom. . . .

It is perhaps not surprising that the author found no indication whatever, from his observations of the teachers in classroom
situations, that as a group those teachers who had had the benefit
of "special education" courses were any "better" teachers than
those who had not.

TEACHER ATTITUDES TOWARD AND SUGGESTIONS FOR THE MASS EDUCATION OF THE RETARDED

What do the teachers feel are the prospects for initiating a
program of mass education for the retarded in the future?

Int.: . . . and obviously a handful of teachers can't handle
it (the mass education of six million retarded children and
adults). You'd need more teachers and I suppose that means
more standardization. You'd have to get some way to educate the retarded en masse.

Teacher: Well, I don't think it would work. I just don't. I
don't see how it can be anything but pretty much an individual thing. This is why I always scream when I get more
than twelve kids. You know legally you can have up to
eighteen. But if you really try to do an adequate job, you
cannot do it with eighteen. You just cannot. I don't care
how many hours at night you put in; it's difficult enough to
do it with twelve. . . . The kids in a so-called normal class are
more alike within the group I think. Our kids, this class I
have, show more differences within the group than a group
of thirty-five so-called normal kids. I have kids who are not
even able to do pre-primer reading. And yet there are
other kids who can do reading fairly well at a fourth grade
level. Well, that's quite a range in a class of thirteen. You
know, and then you have kids who are not even ready for
arithmetic. They're still working on their arithmetic readiness. And other kids are doing things that would be done at
the third or fourth grade level. And then you have everything
in between, you see. You probably wouldn't have this in a
so-called normal class. And the group, at least in our school,
they group them homogeneously too. So you have all the real
bright kids in one group and then the next brightest in another group and so on. . . . So they're, ability-wise, they're
fairly close to being the same.

This teacher's statement fairly well sums up the attitude of
all the teachers interviewed regarding the prospects for mass
education of the retarded as they saw it. It is not surprising that
the teachers themselves were pessimistic, given the state of affairs
outlined above. If mass education for normal children can be
considered successful, it is because there has been some attempt
made to segregate normal children according to age, intellectual
potential, classroom behavior, etc. This has been attempted only
in the grossest terms for the retarded. Categories of "trainable"
and "educable" are hardly adequate distinctions. In education as

in medicine, there is considerable inconsistency in the use of terms. The problems, implicit in the use of I.Q. scores (a favorite indicator among educators for classifying school children, both normal and retarded), has already been discussed in Chapter I. Another example is the use of the term "trainable retarded." The I.Q. range for "trainable" children, as given in a bulletin issued by the Department of Public Instruction, Division of Special Services' Program for Mentally Retarded Children, is 35-50. The characteristics given by the Department for "the trainable mentally handicapped child" are as follows:

1) they (the trainable retarded children)are capable of eventually learning self care in dressing, undressing, eating, toileting, keeping clean, and in other necessary skills which will make them independent of their parents in the regular routines of living;

2) they are capable of learning to get along in the family and in the immediate neighborhood by learning to share, respect property rights, and in general to cooperate with their families or with the neighbors;

3) they are capable of learning to assist in chores around the house or in doing a routine task for some remuneration in a sheltered environment and under supervision;

4) their mental development is approximately one-quarter to one-half that of an average child;

5) *they are generally not capable of learning academic skills such as reading and arithmetic beyond the rote learning of some words or simple numbers* (emphasis added);

6) their speech and language abilities are distinctly limited;

7) they can eventually learn to protect themselves from common dangers; and

8) they will require some care, supervision and economic support throughout their lives.[13]

A key feature of these characteristics, as they relate to educational programs for the retarded and a way of distinguishing the "trainable" from the "educable," is the fact that trainable retarded children are presumed incapable of learning to read with comprehension. Apart from the contentions of the above authoritative source, it seems that trainable retarded children are able to learn to read with comprehension. One of the teachers of an experimental "enriched environment program" for ten mongoloid children at a state residence facility had this to say:

> They are literally reading. For the eight-year-olds, the highest I.Q. is a little bit above fifty. The low . . . nine of the ten children are reading. One little boy is nowhere near it. We're been very unsuccessful with him. The lowest I.Q. involved in the reading is in the low thirties which is phenomenal. *And these children are reading with comprehension.* (Emphasis added)

Categorical distinctions for the "educable" retarded are not much better. The addition of three sub-divisions, i.e. "primary," "intermediate," and "secondary," referring to the segregation of these children into three broad age groups does little to help matters. It is clear that any program of mass education for the retarded will have to classify children according to their existing level of performance and future potential by criteria that are not currently being invoked. This shortcoming is in part a function of the enormous gap in our understanding regarding the current status and/or future potential of the retarded. In this regard, the need is for more research.[14]

However, not all of the current roadblocks to the establishment of a program of mass education for the retarded are based upon ignorance. This aspect has, at least in part, been dealt with earlier. In many regards, we already know what needs to be done to further such a program. Overcoming some of the existing shortcomings of special education programs and the existing nature of teacher-administrator interactions previously outlined by the author, would go a long way in this regard.

In light of the above considerations it is perhaps not surprising to find that there is a common theme among the teachers of the retarded, i.e. that they learn by doing and that there was no particular way to proceed in order to achieve a given end. This is, of course, what one would expect if one's training had little or nothing to do with the task at hand. Teachers were quite explicit in indicating that "Special Education" classes had little or no relevance to the problems of teaching they encountered in a classroom situation. The net result, from the perspective of the teacher, was the failure of "special education" to deal with the problem of educating the retarded, let alone educating them en masse.

This failure, again from the teacher's perspective, was attributable to many factors, e.g. the lack of communication and feedback potential between teacher and student and later between teacher and administrator, the special interests of administrators and/or school districts which retarded the initiation of change, and perhaps more than anything else, the indignation felt by the teachers that those responsible for designing and/or implementing curriculums at the college level for teachers, and at the public school level for students, were persons furthest from the problem and least likely to understand the needs of the children. One teacher put it this way:

> The State is now in the process of developing curriculum for the mentally retarded. They have the guidelines. . . . Districts are supposed to use these guidelines and develop their own programs. But oddly enough, as far as I know, and I've tried to find out, and from what I've been able to find out, there was not one teacher on the committee that developed the guidelines. And here again you have people who do not teach telling the teachers how to teach. And I think it's unrealistic.
> . . . Well, it's just like here, you see, we're observed. My principal was in last week to observe me for an hour. Our consultants observe us all the time. And particularly before you have tenure, you're observed quite closely. And I just kind of resent being observed by somebody who knows less about what I'm doing than I do. I can see where they can make suggestions, you know. They can see things that I'm doing wrong. That's not the point. . . . But very often they look at the thing unrealistically. And so they are critical where maybe they shouldn't be. Now they never have been

with me, so it's not sour grapes. . . . I just don't think that a person who has never taught the mentally retarded can do a good job of evaluating someone who is teaching the mentally retarded, because it's entirely different believe me.

The above statement fairly well sums up the stand of most of the teachers interviewed with regard to their being left out at the planning level. Teacher involvement in the designing of curriculums, apart from achieving a more "realistic" program, would also play a key role in assuring their implementation.[15] The current lack of implementation of special education programs is a serious, and badly overlooked, problem.

A final consideration in an evaluation of educational programs for the retarded leads the author to a discussion of compulsory education. While compulsory education for normal children is taken for granted in the United States, compulsory education for the retarded is not even seriously entertained. This is not true of all countries.

> While compulsory education for normal children in Denmark is only from 7 to 15, children classified as 'mentally deficient' are subject to compulsory education from seven to 21. . . . Compulsory education for the mentally retarded in Sweden is from 7 to 16; in some instances up to the age of 21 (and even 23) at the discretion of the Director of the program and the Central Board.[16]

Not only is education of the retarded compulsory in Denmark and Sweden, but, as in England, there is a national register for the retarded in order to ensure their early identification and assistance.[17] The results of this comprehensive coverage initiated at an early age are heartening.

> One very impressive index of performance attesting the quality of these services is that the infant mortality rate in Sweden in 1959 was 16.6/1000 live births—the lowest in the world. (U.S. infant mortality rate in 1959—26.4/1000 live births.)[18]

Apart from the crucial considerations of life and death, these services provided other impressive benefits to both the retarded

and the community at large. For example, a followup study of
one of the residential institutions for the mentally retarded in
Denmark revealed:

> . . . after leaving this school, 60 percent were able to com-
> pletely care for themselves; 30 percent required some as-
> sistance in the form of counseling, job placement or addi-
> tional training; and ten percent required further institu-
> tional care—apparently because of emotional complications.
> Only six percent of all students discharged from the school
> have come in conflict with the law.[19]

As noted earlier, one key aspect of establishing a program of
mass education for the retarded in this country rests upon training more teachers. One solution to the shortage of teachers needed
for such an undertaking was given by one of the teachers in the
author's series, who is the directress of a kindergarten facility
for retarded children. She recommended the utilization of non-
professional volunteers, i.e. parents, high school students, college
students, or other lay persons, as teachers' aides. The beneficial
effects of such programs have been noted by others[20] and are
already in effect on a very limited scale in both private and public
facilities. I have discussed the use of lay volunteers at the Pre-
school. They were also used even more extensively at the kindergarten. Public schools, with integrated classes for the "educable"
retarded, also used one or two normal children on a volunteer
basis as teachers' aides. However, the directress considered these
efforts "token" and was advocating instead the widespread use
of aides in public school facilities for the retarded. At the same
time, she was not unaware of the problems such a prospect would
pose when she noted the reactions of most teachers to such a
proposal:

> . . . these children, if they are not worked with constantly,
> the minute they're left free to their own devices, many of
> them, particularly the more profoundly involved, just regress
> and will go into whatever their thing is, you know—whatever
> kinesthetic or whatever—and do whatever they have learned
> or used to amuse themselves. So you need a lot of people.

And I find that in working with other teachers—for some reason this is very strange to me—they seem to fear, you know, relinquishing this role as teacher. And they see it only in terms of relating and teaching children. But I see it as a teacher, that the more people that you can involve in the teaching process, then you can have a lot more people doing the kinds of things that you were doing with a lot of children and then you are more free to actively observe this child and what is happening and make recommendations to the various individuals who are working with them and make recommendations to them and suggestions as to how they can do it better or as to what to do next. And I think that all teachers have got to come around, particularly those in special education . . . that if they're going to do a really quality job, and you know certainly meet the needs of these children, and this is true of kinds—this is true of all teachers, that you're going to have to be really welcoming and open your doors to a lot of different kinds of people and not be so protective of, you know, this kind of job.

The widespread use of teachers' aides on an in-training basis is, of course, nothing new. The reluctance of the professional teacher, who feels her autonomy impinged upon or her status threatened, can be overcome. Such programs are already commonplace in other countries.[21] However, the above suggestion of how to recruit more help into educational programs for the retarded would not overcome the problems of evaluating the programs, initiating change, etc., already discussed. This would require the addition of some common outlook or at least "guidelines" to which educational programs for the retarded were all subject, as is the case, for example, in Sweden. It is true that the extensive use of teachers' aides cannot in and of itself provide a means of accomplishing a comprehensive program of mass education for the retarded. However, it does offer a good "stop gap" measure, and might in conjunction with a unified outlook, provide the key to a successful future program.

CONCLUSIONS

All of the factors discussed thus far lead the author to take a dim view of the prospect for mass education of the retarded in this country in the foreseeable future. This would be particularly tragic, given the obvious need for it. The President's Panel on Mental Retardation in 1962 made these recommendations for a comprehensive program of services for the retarded:

1. That programs for the retarded, including modern day care, recreation, residential services, and ample educational and vocational opportunities, be *comprehensive*.
2. That they operate in or close to the communities where the retarded live—that is, that they be *community centered*.
3. That services be so organized as to provide a central or fixed point for the guidance, assistance, and protection of retarded persons if and when needed, and to assure a sufficient array or *continuum* of services to meet different types of need.
4. That private agencies as well as public agencies at the local, state, and Federal level continue to provide resources and to increase them for this worthy purpose. While the Federal Government can assist, the principal responsibility for financing and improving services for the mentally retarded must continue to be borne by States and local communities.[22]

As things now stand, we are nowhere near realizing any, let alone all, of these recommendations. To be able to ultimately succeed in such a program and meet an obvious and distressing need for mass education for the retarded would require a re-evaluation of current State and local educational structures and practices, in order to overcome the hindrances discussed above. There are, of course, other factors forestalling the realization of such a program, not the least of which is inadequate funding. In the words of one teacher:

Every year we go through the same thing. And it gets damn tiring, you know. Really you lose all kinds of patience. Every kid (normal kid) in our building is automatically scheduled for PE, for shop or sewing or cooking, and for music, art and all these things. Ours are not. Every year we have to fight for it *and if there's a cut-back anywhere, ours are the ones that are cut.* (Emphasis added)

These problems will have to be squarely met before there is any real hope for a successful National program. Given the current administration's "austerity" program toward education in the State of California, as well as cutbacks at the national level resulting from the war effort, the prospect for achieving a program of mass education for the retarded in the foreseeable future is not heartening. Whether or not this state of affairs persists remains to be seen. The author can only hope that if there is a shift in the direction of realizing a comprehensive program of public education for the retarded, the recognition and open discussion of existing problems will have had some effect upon bringing it about.

FOOTNOTES—CHAPTER II

1. *Report of the Mission to Denmark and Sweden,* The President's Panel on Mental Retardation, Washington D.C.: Government Printing Office, 1962, p. 17.
2. Mark Conkling, "Sartre's Refutation of the Freudian Unconscious," *Review of Existential Psychology and Psychiatry,* 8 (2), Spring 1968, pp. 95-96.
3. Sarane S. Boocock, "Toward a sociology of learning: A selective review of existing research," *Sociology of Education,* 39 (1), Winter 1966, pp. 5-6.
4. Herbert Sorenson, *Psychology in Education.* New York: McGraw-Hill, 1954, pp. 328-329.
5. Burton Blatt, "Measuring and modifying behavior of special education teachers," *Mental Retardation,* 2(6), 1964, pp. 339-340.
6. The estimate of six million retarded is based upon the figure given by the *President's Panel* that 3% of the country's total population, now at 200,000,000 is retarded. *President's Panel on Mental Retardation,* A Proposed Program for National Action to Combat Mental Retardation, Washington, D.C. Government Printing Office, 1962, p. 1.
7. Robert B. Edgerton, *Cloak of Competence.* Berkeley: University of California Press, 1967, p. 5.
8. Blatt, *op. cit.,* pp. 340-341.
9. George Albee, "Needed a revolution in caring for the retarded," *Trans-Action,* February, 1968, pp. 2-7.
10. This estimate was given by the head of special education classes at a local state college upon addressing an audience of doctors on the topic of education for the retarded.

88   THE SEARCH FOR HELP

11. See, for example, the following:
    Joseph D. Teicher and Jerry Jacobs, "The physician and the adolescent suicide attempter," *Journal of School Health*, 36 (9), 1966, p. 411.
    J. H. Bossard and E. S. Boll, *The Sociology of Child Development*. New York: Harper and Brothers, 1960, p. 435.
    E. Hurlock, *Child Development*. New York: McGraw Hill, 1964, p. 421.
12. Peter M. Blau, *Bureaucracy in Modern Society*. New York: Random House, 1956, pp. 59-61.
13. From a bulletin titled: Department of Public Instruction, Division of Special Services, Program for Mentally Retarded Children, circulated by San Francisco State College, San Francisco, California, pp. 1-2.
14. President's Panel, *op. cit.*, pp. 31-32.
15. John H. Johansen, "'The relationship between teachers' perceptions of influence in local curriculum decision making and curriculum implementation," *The Journal of Education Research*, 61(2), 1967, p. 82.
16. Report of the Mission to Denmark and Sweden, *op. cit.*, p. 12.
17. *Ibid.*, p. 15.
18. *Ibid.*, p. 15.
19. *Ibid.*, pp. 19-20.
20. W. M. Cruickshank and N. C. Haring, *A Demonstration: Assistants For Teachers of Exceptional Children*. Syracuse: Syracuse University Press, 1957.
21. Report of the Mission to Denmark and Sweden, *op. cit.*, p. 29.
22. President's Panel, *op. cit.*, p. 15.

CHAPTER III

The Child's Effect Upon the Family: Current Anxieties and Future Expectations

WE HAVE ALREADY considered in the opening chapter some of the life and death decisions made by parents of retarded children. The parents' contemplation of infanticide as a means of sparing the child and the family future problems that they felt were sure to develop as a result of the child's retardation, is, of course, of great import. Its greater significance, however, lies in the fact that it is a specific instance of the general case of "what will it all (the extended effort and suffering on the part of parents, sibs, and retarded child) come to anyway?"

INFANTICIDE

Entertaining the notion of infanticide was in no way peculiar to the parents in the author's series.[1] For example, a parent in the study by Brice and Bartelme states the following:

> I never really planned to kill my child, but I have thought of how much easier it would be if he died; my religion is the only thing that keeps me from killing my child.[2]

If religion kept some parents from murdering their retarded child, it may have served for others as a means of constructing the moral justification of infanticide.

> The Reverend Mr. Sholin . . . said his son, Edward Allen, suffered brain damage when his oxygen supply was curtailed

just before birth. The minister said after being told the infant would be 'something close to an inanimate object,' he decided to take his pediatrician's advice and remove his son from an oxygen tent. The infant died three days later.

The Reverend went on to say:

Tragic decisions like this one are made every day. I believe that the people who have to make them, under the proper circumstances, should no longer be lawbreakers. (Emphasis added.)

The article also noted that:

. . . while still 'burdened' by his decision (to let his son die), he (the minister) would do the same thing today.[3]

The altruistic murder of the mentally retarded is noted elsewhere.[4] D. J. West cites four cases of murder-suicide involving a parent's murder of a retarded child, followed by the suicide of the parent.[5] Forty-seven percent of a total of 148 cases of murder-suicide studied by West were instances of parents killing their own children.[6]

One mother in the author's series recounted her contemplation of murder-suicide as follows:

A year ago, we (the mother and child) reached a crisis. When her behavior went so haywire, when things were so bad, you mentioned Sonoma, that I was on the verge of committing the child and because that was so intolerable, I thought that perhaps suicide and homicide together would be a better solution for her and for me. And it sounds awful, but it is an alternative. And it is one way. If you can't do what's necessary and you can't buy it, you can't ask it, you can't beg it, it's like if there's nothing on TV, simply nothing. Even people who are completely hung up on TV will sometimes turn the damn set off. And I just considered, you know, that turning her off and turning myself off because I couldn't bear to live after that, might be the, you know, best thing. That's how bad things were.

Conditions have improved markedly and unexpectedly for this family within the last year, and the mother no longer entertains murder-suicide as a possible solution to her and the child's problems. In fact, things are so much better that the mother now states she is able "to live with it."

Another mother had this to say about the prospect of her son surviving her and her husband. Here, as in all the verbatim accounts, much is lost in transcription. To have heard the inflection in the mother's voice and seen the sheepish expression on her face as she spoke the words would have left the listener with little room for ambiguity when she said:

> . . . I wouldn't want Norman to live until he's forty without John (her husband) and I being there to go through it with him. I don't know what he would do. I feel this way—if Norman outlives us, please God take him with us when we go. Because I mean that's the way I want things. I don't want him . . . I don't want him . . . If John and I can't keep him with us all through life, until it goes one way or the other, if we're taken before he is, like I said, I want him to go with us. If he's taken before us, then we are ready to accept it. Because if he goes through life with us, if all of a sudden we're not here tomorrow, he's going to be in a terrible state of shock. And of course if they throw him in a colony again, or a state hospital, then that might even be worse than anything else. So it might actually be better if Norman were taken with us if we go before he does. I mean that's the way I feel about it. Many other people might not agree with me. But I do. I believe that a retarded child has just as much right to live as a normal child, but I don't want to see them living in a miserable way.

A third parent who felt at one point that it would be a "blessing" to let her retarded child die gave this account:

> . . . sometimes my husband will call me during the day and we talk on the phone and I tell him, you know, a lot of things that were upsetting me and I wouldn't tell anyone else, the things that I tell him, you know, we wouldn't share with other people, the kinds of things we share with each other,

feelings about Paul, and for a long time we wished he would die, because well, we would have regarded it a blessing. Of course this comes kind of naturally because a good section of our society regards the death of a retarded child as a blessing. It is a common reaction . . . I mean there was . . . one time I was giving him food and he wasn't eating it or taking food, he was about two; he had a respiratory infection—he was very ill for days and I was giving him fluid by rectum and I found myself thinking at the time, gee I wish he'd just die—but I couldn't do that, you know, I could not make that last effort.

The author has already noted in the first chapter a fourth mother who thought of smothering her retarded child and attributing it to a "crib death."

INSTITUTIONAL CARE

A key factor in the benevolent view that parents of retarded children took toward infanticide revolved around the prospect of their ultimately having to institutionalize their child. This sentiment was clearly expressed in the above accounts. The general feeling was—why let the child live and the family suffer if all that results is that the child is finally "put away"? The despair that was felt by parents of retarded children at this prospect was based upon their low opinion of institutional care, i.e., parents tended to see an institutional setting for their retarded child as a "dead end." Once the child was institutionalized, parents felt there was no hope for his future development. In fact, it was generally believed that his condition was likely to deteriorate. One parent, the only one in the author's series who had her child institutionalized at one point and removed him from "residence care" after a period of six months, had this to say about her experience:

So when Lucy, my third child, was born, it was a few months later in January when Norman was a year and a half that we took him to X Children's Colony, and he was there for six months. It's something like X State Hospital. He couldn't adjust and he was getting sick and was sick for the six months he was there. And so it was on our last visit that we seen just how bad he was doing. He wasn't improving at all and was getting worse. He had lost weight. He forgot how to walk. He couldn't hardly crawl. I mean what color he had when he was put in there was all gone. And so we thought that by having him there, it was more or less killing him.

In this case, the process of having their child institutionalized was seen by the parents as tantamount to murder. Had the child died while in the "colony" the parents would have felt responsible for his death. Nor in one sense was this an unrealistic appraisal. The fact is that since his removal from the institution five and a half years ago, the child has shown constant developmental improvement in all areas—physical, psychological and social.

The parents' concern for their retarded child's welfare in institutional settings was not without good grounds. One expert in the field drew this parallel.

> Literally, more money is publicly expended on the care of animals in our zoos than in the care of human beings in our state institutions. I have studied five of our largest zoos and find that they average $7.15 per capita daily cost for the care and feeding of animals of human size. The most recent survey of the United States Department of Health, Education, and Welfare this past August (1967) reports a per capita daily expenditure of $6.71 per patient under treatment in public institutions for the mentally retarded.[7]

An article reporting on a recent "confidential" study of state mental retardation facilities conducted by a team of experts from the California Medical Association and "pried" loose for public consumption revealed the following:

> SONOMA—'Drastically overcrowded . . . Built for 2400 patients, it now houses over 3400.' The understaffed maintenance department is facing a crisis. Building and interior repair work is at least five years behind current needs. Few teachers are available for the mentally retarded children. Their schooling is neglected. Staff standards are low. 'The only dental care made available is emergency extractions.'

NAPA—Patients receive less staff time than before (before current administrative cutbacks). The staff shortage is most noticeable in the children's wards. The size of the group therapy sessions has been increased fifty percent. The food is drab and sometimes served cold. 'Many patients spend time looking after other patients. It is incongruous that many of these patients have all or part of their costs paid by their families, insurance policies, estates, etc., but they receive no remuneration for this alleged work therapy . . .'[8]

The article is too long to include in its entirety. Suffice it to say that the above was not unrepresentative of the conditions found in most of the other state institutions for the retarded considered in the study.

Some statistical indication of current inadequacies in public institutions for the mentally retarded on a national level is found in the 1968 report of the President's Committee on Mental Retardation. It is indicated that residents reported overcrowding in 75% of all the larger institutions. With respect to staffing, the report indicates that there are half or less than half the number of staff required in the following occupational categories: attendants, registered nurses, social workers and psychologists. In addition, there is a shortage of 2,300 occupational therapists, 2,900 physical therapists, and 5,100 medical social workers. The salaries of many attendants at institutions for the retarded were below poverty levels. These were only a few of the areas of crucial shortages noted in the report.[9]

Some idea of what former adult institutionalized retardates thought of their institutionalization can be had from the following accounts:

Martha recalls her stay at Pacific as one of unrelieved misery. In the first place, she felt exploited: 'Nobody paid me anything. I did all that work every day and never got one cent. They just kept us smarter patients there because if it wasn't for us who'd do the work? The employees wouldn't do it. They just stand around and make the patients work.'

But she also felt fear and the loss of freedom. 'I was just like an animal in a cage. Bars and all. And anytime you did something they didn't like they'd threaten you with punishment like being locked up in a side room all alone. That's what they'd do, you know. They'd drug me with narcotics, like amdol (amytal), then put me in a room all alone. How is a person going to live right when they're full of narcotics? . . . The problem is that when you have been locked away in there for a long time you get nervous and also you don't learn about how to live outside, so when you get outside you can't act like a normal person—even when you're smarter than outside people. I was in there so long I thought I was going to rot. It's not right. I never belonged there and then they kept me so long that now I'm confused and nervous and can't get a job. All my troubles come from being in that place."[10]

Another former patient felt this way about it:

Mary went to school at Pacific for about a year and was able to improve her reading and writing considerably. Moreover, her IQ score increased in this period from 44 to 56. She was given jobs in the hospital and learned to care for children and to perform simple housekeeping tasks. She was never a troublemaker and got along quite well with the employees. She also lived fairly happily with the other patients in her 'cottage,' where she made many friends among the girls of her age.

Despite such generally pleasant experiences, Mary was usually very unhappy in the hospital and was always anxious to leave it . . . She resented her loss of freedom, privacy and individuality; she disliked some of the girls in the institution, especially the homosexuals; she felt that the food was not fit to eat; she was disappointed to discover that there was no swimming pool or riding stable as she had been led to believe. She wanted to leave Pacific as soon as possible.[11]

Edgerton had this to say about the mortification of patients during their initial period of hospitalization:

. . . entry into Pacific State Hospital presents the retarded person with a new dilemma. Although he is by now thoroughly familiar with mortification and has probably developed means of self defense against suggestions of mental deficit, he is surely not prepared for the experiences that the hospital will inflict upon him. The cumulative impact of the initial period of hospitalization (at the time of the research) was greatly mortifying, leaving the patient without privacy, without clear identity, without autonomy of action, without relatives, friends, or family in a regimented and impersonal institution where everything combines to inform him that he is, in fact, mentally inadequate. A typical patient reaction is seen in the following words of a teenage boy who was newly admitted to the institution: 'Why do I got to be here with these people? I'd rather be dead than here.'[12]

Edgerton goes on to note that even after the initial adjustment period,

the patients seldom appreciated either the hospital confinement or its regulations. As a result, *freedom from institutional confinement was a primary goal for every patient in the cohort*.[13] (Emphasis added.)

An interesting contrast to the mortification that adult retardates experienced upon being institutionalized, and their universal desire to be free at the earliest opportunity, is reported in a recent article in the *Wall Street Journal*.

Three of every four adults living in this tiny village at the end of a winding Yorkshire country lane are mentally handicapped. . . . Botton is neither an institution nor a mental hospital, at least in the usual sense of the terms. It is a small town representing an unusual approach to an often neglected field. Here, handicapped adults live, work and participate in their own community . . . Decision-making, though often nothing more momentous than choosing a new color for a room, is open to them. And everybody here has a job. . . . 'Our aim is not to rehabilitate the handicapped into the outside world but to give them a permanent life here,' says Mrs. Jean Talle, a staff member. As a result, Botton and a handful of similar villages around the world started by persons trained here have evolved as secluded, nearly self-contained societies. They claim to be free of the competitive atmosphere that makes it difficult for mentally handicapped to get along in the outside world. . . . Many handicapped have left the village, improved enough to live on the outside. . . . Most village residents, though free to leave, would prefer not to, and at least half of the ninety handicapped here now will live their lives in Botton. . . . Life is informal. Everyone is on a first name basis, and no one gets paid for work . . . 'We are prepared to live with the handicapped. They find their recognition. The isolation we have is because they need a sheltered social and work environment.' . . . The staffers work hard to avoid being proctors. No walls surround Botton. This has caused problems on occasion, . . . but staff members dismiss this as the price to pay for avoiding the mental hospital atmosphere. . . .[14]

Nor should Botton be seen as an isolated "Utopia." It gives every indication of becoming a small scale international movement.

Botton, which received much of its financial support from the British government, became a successful operation. Two more villages were put up in Britain, and one each was established in Germany, South Africa and Switzerland. In 1962, a Botton-trained worker organized a village at Copake, New York, . . .[15]

The author feels that the orientation towards retardation described above is, at least for some categories of the retarded, a step in the right direction. Many have paid lip service to such an outlook, but little has been done, at least in this country, to implement it. Some may take exception to the notion of an isolated self-contained society. But is this any different than the "total institution"[16] found at any large state facility for the retarded? Others may question the wisdom of not aiming to rehabilitate the patient. However, the article notes that, "many handicapped have left the village, improved enough to live outside . . ." The question may be asked: How many institutionalized adult retardates are sufficiently "rehabilitated" to live "outside"? Edgerton noted only 110 adults who "graduated" between 1949 and 1958 at an institution that had some 3,000 patients at the time of the study.[17]

In the final analysis, the key differences seem to be that the retarded described in the article, because of the different practices and goals of that setting, seem not to have been subject to a process of mortification and although free to leave (unlike the adults in Edgerton's sample) chose not to. I feel that these points alone are a compelling testimonial to the relative merits of such a program, at least as a stop-gap measure during the transition period to more comprehensive programs for the retarded.

Keeping in mind all of the above, it is perhaps not surprising to find that parents placed their retarded children in institutions only as a last resort and usually with the understanding that it was more for the family's benefit than the child's.[18] Whether or not the press of necessity was felt early in the child's life or later depended upon a great many circumstances, e.g. the availability of outside help, family size, the parents' financial resources, the psychological makeup of the parents, etc. However, at whatever point the parents filed an application and got on a waiting list to have their child institutionalized, it was usually done only as a backup measure "just in case" or, in the final analysis, as a last resort. Kramm had this to say about the attitude of parents of mongoloid children toward the prospect of institutionalizing their children:

> Not until they felt convinced within themselves that it was necessary for their child's future security could they even consider the idea of placing him.[19]

The reader is asked to note the distinction between "future security" and future development. In the above regard, Kramm reports the following findings:

> When the parents were asked what they thought an institution could do for a retarded child, only fifteen of the one hundred mentioned special benefits; some of these thought he might receive better training and supervised recreation; others, that he would have round-the-clock supervision, good medical care, and the companionship of 'his own kind.' Fifty

parents said that an institution had no advantage except to give shelter to the child after the parents were dead. Twenty-two others stated flatly that the institution could do nothing at all for the retarded child. Thirteen had no opinion; they had never thought about an institution in connection with their child.

But regardless of what the parents thought the institution could or could not do for the retarded child, twenty-three families had filed their first application for placement. In thirteen of these families, neither parent had ever visited an institution for retarded children. This was also the case in nineteen of the twenty-seven families that had not filed an application. Among those who had applied were ten families in which the parents could not agree about placement. Only two of these twenty parents had ever gone to see the place where their child might be sent.[20]

Given the nature of care in institutions for the retarded and the parents' early recognition of these inadequacies, most parents were under considerable strain waiting to see if their child's future development would ultimately necessitate placement. Since the children at the Pre-school were between the ages of four and eight, and the usual cautious predictions of doctors and other experts regarding the child's potential for future development was "wait and see" (in fact, wait until the child was about twelve), the parents usually became anxious early in the child's life about what to expect of him as an adolescent.

Well . . . it's hard to tell (how far the child will develop). I've been waiting for that. In fact, every ah, ah, he sees the doctor two and three times a year unless an emergency, but ah, Doctor Jones has been seeing him on the average of two and three times a year. And that's a question I'd always ask him. Could you tell us now how far will Louis go—cause he does different things with Louis. And he sees a difference in him. I says well now, and he says Mrs. S. he says it's hard to tell. He says really he says I'll tell you maybe when he's ah eight years old. Well maybe I can't tell you anything till he's ten or eleven twelve. That's as far as he went. Twelve was the furtherest. So, my husband and I have in mind we're going to wait until Louis is twelve. They should tell us by then if he's going to go any further or he'll be lower or what.

"LEARNING TO LIVE WITH IT"

The question arises—what did parents do while awaiting future clues to their child's development? For the most part, parents in the author's series adopted a policy of "not thinking too far ahead" or "going day to day" as a strategy for "learning to live with it." One pre-school mother put it this way:

You, you don't know what it's going to be like in the future. You, you have to think about it a little bit but it can get a little frightening at times . . . thinking about the future. So John (her retarded child) has taught me one other lesson of how to take things as they come and live from day to day. And that you really can't plan that far in advance.

Another added:

No. See I go day by day and month by month. But I'm not going to sit—like when they interviewed me before, (they asked) what are you going to do when you have to tell her she's going to become a woman? I'll worry about that at the time. When the time comes, then we'll take care of that situation. I'm not going to sit down and . . . she's only seven now. Am I going to sit down for the next nine years and think, what am I going to do and all that stuff? Let nature take its course in time. Time heals everything, and I figure work day for day, month for month. Take care of things as it comes.

A third parent, in summing up her primary concern with the concrete everyday problems of the here and now, had this to say:

They used to say things to me like—do you feel guilty, (about having a retarded child)? Are you disappointed? Disappointed? Guilty? Christ if I could just get a bottle down her. It's much more real, Dr. Jacobs. It's not all this theory. It's really not as psychological. It's . . . it's solid. It's something, you have to deal with it like you have to deal with this table. Are you going to sit on it, under it, beside it . . . (you deal with it) day by day, it isn't . . . you don't look so much, especially in the first few years, to the future. You can't imagine your child five feet tall, weighing 130 pounds and punching boys in the nose. You don't think of that. It's a tiny thing. It's five, seven, eight, ten pounds, thirteen pounds in one year. Many of these children are undersized. It's even harder to imagine them growing up. They don't grow up. So why should you think of their growing up? No, it was the effort of lifting her over and over and over again out of the crib. And putting her down and praying she would sleep, and begging to any god that existed, even Satan, if she would only sleep.

The notion that retarded children fail to grow up leads the author to a consideration of how this tends to further restrict parents of retarded children to a present-oriented time perspective. We have already noted that the child's future career was defined by professionals as ambiguous, e.g., "he might not develop beyond the six-year-old level," and that the acceptance of this assessment by the parents led to the further prospect that the child might ultimately have to be institutionalized, or that the parents might die and leave the child stranded, helpless in a hostile world. The accumulation of such prospects was for the parents overwhelming. As such, they were avoided in self defense and helped to minimize—for the parents—any consideration of the child's future and to orient them instead toward the here and now.

Another factor working to orient the parents toward the present was the idea that retarded children fail to grow up. This notion is so pervasive that it is difficult even for professionals to overcome it. The author, during a number of field trips to various homes and workshops for adult retardates and state facilities with adult wards, was struck by the fact that dedicated and well-meaning nurses, technicians, teachers, social workers and vocational rehabilitation counsellors, all consistently referred to thirty- or forty-year old retarded adults as "the kids." With the professional as with the parent, such an orientation probably tends to leave the helping agent with the feeling that the child "does not have much of a future." One pre-school mother expressed it this way:

> . . . It is a blessing in a lot of ways (having a retarded child). You have a child who is, you have a child who is home longer, who is a baby longer. Everybody always says oh I wish they could stay babies a little longer. . . . It is nice to have one who will be home longer than the rest of the children. And particularly being that we're growing older.

ADOLESCENCE AND ADULTHOOD

However, the tendency of all of the above forces to negate the child's future were only partially successful. Two main areas of future concern always managed to assert themselves, i.e. the child's future development as an adolescent or adult and the well-being of the child after the death of the parent. The latter was particularly important in generating parental anxiety. The following are some of the parents' accounts regarding their hopes and fears for their child in adolescence and adulthood:

> Well, it's like little wisecracks have been said to me, about some day he's going to be pulling you instead of you pulling him. And it's going to be true, too . . . And if and when Jeffrey does get to the point that he controls us, then he will be put away. I mean, there's a drawer at home that's very handy that's full of butcher knives. Jeffrey never touched it. The first time he does, he's going to wind up very sorry for it. And if and when he learns that he feels like he wants to go around to stab at the kids, and I can't control it, he will be put away. Like I say—when he controls us, I've had it. I won't take no more. It won't be because I don't love him, and it won't be because my husband and I very seriously feel that we've done wrong; it will just be that he's uncontrollable now and that we've done the very best that we could.

> I haven't been able to bring myself to consider that quite yet (the prospect of institutionalizing her son). I think the chances are that he will need to be placed in some kind of

residential situation, and we've kind of accepted that, when he gets to be a teenager and difficult to manage, assuming he doesn't change too much from what he is now since he hasn't changed much in the last five years; I don't expect him to change a lot, you know. I would expect that he probably will need a residential type of situation . . . unless we can control his behavior considerably more than we really can now. I don't think I could manage him.

If he continues at his present rate of development, we have every intention of keeping him at home . . . unless, as I say, I can't foresee the future. If he got to the point where we couldn't control him or something, you know, that might lead to it (having him institutionalized) but other than that we wouldn't consider it. And I don't think it's necessary; he does fine in a family situation.

Oh yes I've thought about it (what her child will be like as an adolescent). Well I hope mentally she develops much better. Cause I thought of her going through the menstrual period with diapers. Now I don't know how that would be. How much she would understand. And how come, you know, it would be a problem too, well, I guess it would be a problem anyway, but with a young lady that doesn't understand. . . . But like I say, it's a long way off.

Well, that was the first trip we made to X school. They had a PTA luncheon, a fund raiser that they have around Christmas time, and they sell things that the children made. . . . So we made a date with them to where we went the following May, and she the principal took us to the different classrooms from the little guys up to the big ones. And then your eyes are opened; you feel the real light. I did, and I'm just hoping that Roy (her retarded son) will be able to do that. . . . And when I told him (her husband) that this 18-year-old boy that reminded me of Roy so much . . . well this little guy, even his coloring reminded me of Roy. I says I picture Roy that old already. Oh, he says, you're sending him off to work already. And this little boy was in the cafeteria, and getting lunch. We stayed there until lunch because we purposely did that because we wanted to see the children. They helped prepare the lunch for, in the cafeteria with the mothers, and it makes you feel a little better, especially when you see a child that's the same as yours that's doing it.

Well, you know, I've learned that . . . you don't think about that (the child as an adult). You know, I often think that the bubble is going to burst, and everyone is going to say that there was never anything really wrong with the child to begin with and everything's going to be perfect. I think we all kind of wish that. And then I think well maybe I'll have him home with me for the rest of my life. He'll be able to do things, but he wouldn't be able to . . . wouldn't like well get married if there's something the matter, depending what it would be. And then I just think I shouldn't think at all, because none of us, none of us can plan . . . I mean there are things that you sort of wait until the time comes. Yeah, well, . . . well sure I used to think well, will he be able to get married, you know, when they said he needs a special school. What, what have I got here? You know, and all that type of thing. And you learn from many of the other mothers who have children with problems that . . . you just don't even think about these things. I think if you think too much (you'll be overwhelmed).

So I guess it's natural that he (the husband) would be (overprotective) because he figures that she (the retarded child) can't defend herself as well as . . . Of course he's always, even with the older girls with dating, he is always very very strict because you know, he felt that there was so much harm could come. Well, God knows it happens all the time. You see the terrible things that happen, you've just got to pick up the newspaper. But he worries all the time about her, very much so. And in fact we had an interview with Dr. Jones (who) invited us to go up to Stockton last summer to be interviewed by a group of public health nurses. And some of these women brought up, such as we hadn't thought of

before—at least I hadn't thought of before—marriage. . . .
I just took it for granted that she wouldn't, . . . well, I know
retarded children who are in their thirties, and they're still
living at home, and they're perfectly content. So I just kind
of figured that this was the pattern that most retarded
people followed, well unless they were institutionalized. And
one of the people, I don't remember if it was Dr. Jones or one
of the nurses, said—and just what do you see for Joanne in
the future? And he says, well he says, I think she'll probably
get married. And gee, I, you know, we've never talked about
it. We've never talked about this kind of thing. . . . Well, I've
done a great deal of thinking about that since that time. And
in fact, I've talked with other people about it, Mrs. H. in
particular (the Pre-school director) . . . and she told me of
a young couple that she heard of that were both of them retarded, and they wanted to get married, but they felt it was
inadvisable to have children and the girl was sterilized. So
under those circumstances, why I guess this would, you
know, like my husband was saying, well with birth control
pills, you know who needs to worry about having children.
But of course we're Catholic, which kind of . . . right now
we're kind of under a cloud as far as this is concerned, as
far as birth control pills and as far as sterilization is concerned, because the church does not allow sterilization even
for people who are mentally retarded . . . I had never thought
of her getting married, although I think that Joanne might be
a very good housewife, she loves to help around the house,
set the table, and do things . . . and she loves babies—oh she
dearly loves babies.

THE CARE OF THE CHILD UPON THE
DEATH OF THE PARENTS

We have already given some indication of the problems that
face parents of retarded children. Would their child become unmanageable in adolescence or adulthood and have to be institutionalized? Would they be able to find future educational facilities? Would they marry and/or have children or be partially self-
sufficient? These were all future problems that parents of retarded
children struggled with. However, perhaps more important than
these with respect to the ability of future concerns to generate

current anxiety, was the question of what would become of the child upon the death of the parents. This problem was one that parents often considered but rarely discussed with others. Then, too, they found small solace in such discussions on the rare occasions that the topic arose. The parents' expression of this problem and their inability to resolve it is illustrated below in a sampling from the transcribed verbatim accounts:

Ooooh! Oh yes. Heavens, Yes. (She had thought about what would become of her child in the event of her death). Boy, one day something happened to me and I can remember the block in which I was walking, you know, and it occurred to me then I must have had a very sharp pain, I can't really tell you what happened to me, because I don't remember. But it gave rise to certain emotions, you know, and that was the first thing I thought about. And I didn't give one thought to my other two children. That was the first thing I thought about. If I am not around and . . . and I still tell myself that, you know. These two (her normal children) can take care of themselves. . . . But Patricia, if something happens to me, what about Patricia? Who's going to take care of Patricia? Oh . . . I used to, oh boy, I'll tell you, that really was always uppermost in my mind and it still bothers me. But as I think about that right now, I don't think about that nearly as much as I used to. And I think it's because I see evidence of the progress that she's making. But that used to bother me—oh that particular day I actually started praying that nothing would—and I pray that prayer all the time, that I might live to see her grown, because I really don't know, I have every hope that she's going to be all right, but if she isn't, I want to be the one to take care of her you know. I always think about that. That more than anything else. And when I think about that, I never involve my other two kids in that thought. I wonder about that all the time you know. I figure that they've got it made, I guess; I don't know. Which is maybe not the way to feel, but it's always Patricia that I'm thinking about when I think maybe the day will come when I won't be around and then what. I say no don't let that happen, you know, anything but that.

As I say, I intend as long as I am able to keep him at home. And we wrestled this around—whether it's better for our other children. You know, to grow up and take on responsibility for Sam. And I don't think they would have to unless they wanted to as they grew older. So at that point we might have to, possibly we might have to institutionalize him. If something happened to my husband and I. And as I say we wrestled this over whether we should bring up our children with the idea that one of them is going to take over Sam if something ever happened to either of us. But I don't know if it's fair to them. Because they're entitled to a life of their own. It's not their fault they have a retarded brother. That's why my husband felt we should at least put in an application in the event that it ever becomes necessary (to have him institutionalized). And this is kind of like saying—what are you gonna have for dinner next Wednesday? Who knows where I'll be next Wednesday? You know, this is sort of a far fetched thing, but I think it's one of our biggest worries.

Yeah, what do we do with Mike? How far do you go with him? Of course, the big thing we take everything and just kind of go along with it. But the big thing is if something happens to my husband and I, then what is there for Mike? That's the big big problem, because the brothers and sisters won't be able to take him. Because he's mine and he's my husband's, and we take care of him—they're a lot of care. And there are a lot of people who just can't cope with them.

I sort of dread it, but well the only time I was real frustrated about Janet going to Sonoma, I talked to Dr. Black and Dr. Smith, and Mrs. H. was the only one who I think sort of knocked me to my senses that day. Cause I was really considering it, because I thought if it was best for Janet then this was what I wanted. But I wasn't sure that this was best for Janet. I wanted to go see what Sonoma was like . . . and I said well what would happen to her if we died? And she (Mrs. H.) said well, she would automatically go to Sonoma. And I didn't know this. She said there is something

called an emergency something or other. But I couldn't
ask her godmother to take her. But the more I think about
it she might change. But I believe she would take her. Although I never really discussed it with her. But it would be,
I don't know, now that I think about it, it starts me to
feeling that way again. . . . But then you wonder—okay, as
things stand now, they say they're understaffed and over-
crowded and oh there are so many things, nightmares you
can have about somebody beating your child. Or a bad
mental case, maybe vicious who'll maybe grab her and hurt
her, oh a lot of things you think about that are frustrating.
And at the same time you're hoping that it doesn't happen
but you really don't know.

———————————

And I immediately thought well, what's going to become of
her? This was the first thing that entered my mind. I don't
know whether it's because I'm older, and I suppose if it
were my first child or even my second I might have gotten
more upset, but having four for myself, I wasn't shocked
(to learn that she had a retarded child). I thought well, those
things happen, why should it be any different for me? We'd
had a good life and all the breaks up till that time. That
didn't upset me. But what did upset me was the fact that
she had had elderly parents, or they would be elderly in no
time at all. And this still bothers me. This is my big concern.

———————————

Yeah, we've thought about this quite a lot. In fact, we've
thought about it from the standpoint of both the children;
my husband has been talking for years about making a will
and setting up some sort of guardian procedure for David.
We would like to set it up in such a way that if anything
happened to us, we're going to make reciprocal wills with
my sister, and that if anything happens to them, we would
take the children, and if anything happened to us, they would
take the children, but we wanted to make provision for
David to be admitted immediately to say Sonoma, so they
wouldn't have to worry about that, you know. . . . Where
Mary could be absorbed easily with my sister's two year
olds, David would be considerably more of a problem. . . .

So anyway, we've been going to do this for a number of years. I don't know why we didn't get around to doing it. It's a funny thing—this business of making a will. I guess you, it's sort of the thing you don't really think about *really* needing, and although we've talked about it a lot, we just haven't done it yet.

But like I say our problem is what's going to become of Charlotte, if something happens to us? Where will she end up? And nobody's given me an answer. . . . You never know. You can be healthy today and . . . I've given it a lot of thought; like I say we both think but we don't know what to do. We just don't know what to do or who to turn to.

Here again, the above concern was in no way peculiar to the parents in the author's study. The following are a few illustrations from the verbatim accounts of the parents in Kramm's series:

The only thing that worries his father and me is what will happen to Alex if anything happens to us. This is more recent thinking because the mister and I are getting along. His dad has always thought of his future. I'm sure that is the reason why, just as soon as we knew about Alex, he took out a 20-year policy for him. And we've never tried to put him away. We want to keep him home. He's not a bad child. I'm strong. I don't mind doing for him. Still, we can't expect his brothers and sisters to take care of him.

We want to see what we can do for Bob—if we can manage. All the relatives say keep him—don't let him be taken away. We have all learned to love him. We'll keep him as long as we can. We applied for care to give Bob security only because we hate the thought of his being left out if we die.

. . . Earlier, I thought he would grow up to be a comfort to me. Now, we have to coax him so long it's hardly worth while. I hope we'll outlive him or all go together. I wish he could be placed in a happy individualized atmosphere, near home, before I die. . . . We'd never dump him on our other children or suggest they take care of him. If they suggested it, that would be different, but they have their own life to live and we keep out of it. The thing now is to find a place for Malcolm. If there's money, that's possible. But we'd miss him if he were gone.[21]

The practitioner's awareness of the serious and ubiquitous nature of this problem and his free and open discussion of it with the parents, would go a long way toward providing a much needed and sought after relief.

The anxiety generated by the uncertainty of what would become of the child upon the death of the parents was only one of a series of effects that the retarded child had upon the family. The following discussion will consider some additional ones in two sections: the effects upon the parents and the effects upon the sibs.

EFFECTS UPON THE PARENTS

The literature relating to the effects of the child's retardation upon the parents is divided into essentially two camps. One group of researchers feels that fathers make a faster and/or better adjustment to the child's retardation than mothers do.[22] Another group believes the opposite.[23] The author's data very definitely favors the latter view. Most fathers in the author's series (according to the mothers' accounts) were less able to accept the diagnosis, tried to hide the fact that they had a retarded child from the public, and/or were more often overprotective. The following are a series of relevant excerpts from the verbatim accounts as they relate to the effects of the child's retardation upon the father, and their consequences for the father, mother and child.

I don't think he's (the husband) accepted it (the child's retardation) yet. My husband is a very deep man, and he keeps most of his thoughts to himself. He doesn't believe in showing any emotion. And this has hit him harder than he realizes. And his behavior has changed a great deal, and this is quite (clear)—to other people, not only me, but many people have seen it in him. My husband doesn't see it in himself. He's just been the way he is, (he thinks) but there's been a drastic change in him. . . . He used to be quite easy going, and nothing seemed to get to him too much, and he was much happier and much more relaxed. And I mean I don't think he's over Paul yet. He's the type that may never get over it. He's closer to Paul than to any of the other children. Spends all of his time with Paul. And this got to be a problem, because he was spoiling him so much that the pediatrician said—if you ever hope to accomplish anything, he'll have to learn discipline. So the pediatrician wrote a letter to my husband, you know, that he would have to crack down and not let him get away with murder. . . . I don't feel he (the husband) has recouped. He won't even go to a doctor. And I say he's just one of these people who has to hold everything in and thinks emotions are reserved for other people, and he has no real release. . . . And he cannot talk about it very readily. I don't think I've ever heard him say that he has a retarded child. I'm sure the people he works with have no idea that we have a handicapped child.

———————

. . . he (her husband) tries not to see the bad side of it (the child's retardation). He would more or less like to think that there wasn't anything really wrong with John. But as each day went by, we could see it more and more. Not so much the days, but when the months go by, and he makes no improvement, and then we have little nieces and nephews, well we have one niece that was born three weeks before John. And when you put the two of them together, it hits you in the face like a ton of bricks. . . . But that's when it really, uh, you know, you really get the cold facts. There's no ands or buts; it's right there. But my husband didn't say too much. He'll hold more inside than he would let out.

———————

. . . I told Sam, (her husband) I says—I've got to tell the people I'm close to (that she has a retarded child) because I

just can't keep that to myself. . . . That's not solving anything. Well, Sam didn't want to talk about it, so I would
tell them. But myself, I think I'm the luckier of the two
because I can talk about it. . . . Oh sure, yeah, because if it
helps (talking to someone else about it) I hope that it will
help my husband. This is what I'm hoping more than for myself. Because like I said I probably need a lot of help, but
I'm able to talk about it more. If they say—how's Herbert
(her retarded son), I don't clam up. Sam doesn't do that as
much any more. At first, people were almost afraid to ask
him—how's Herbert. Because they could just see the tension
in him; that's not good. You can't, you know, live that way.
. . . I guess it bothers me in different ways than it bothers
him or something. I just feel that you kind of have to take
it as it comes.

Well, it's rather interesting (what her husband thought
about the child's retardation). I don't think he felt there
was anything wrong with him at all. . . . When I first mentioned to him that there might be something wrong, I wasn't
quite sure how to put it, because this baby meant everything
in the world to him. I mean, you know, like he felt like the
king of the road. This was the culmination of all his hopes
and dreams—to have a son. And I suggested to him that I
hoped he wouldn't be too disappointed if it turned out that
Robert was maybe not able to go to med school. And he
was quite upset when I mentioned that. He was really angry.
He said—well, I never said I wanted him to be a doctor.
He really reacted to that. And I, you know, actually I didn't
think Robert was really terribly impaired at that point. I
was just wondering if maybe he might not be quite as bright
as we thought. Maybe he would never make it to college. . . .
But I had a hunch he (the husband) would have had some
kind of special goals for him.

And my husband is the kind that likes the voice of authority
. . . and this was authority (the doctor's advice to the parents
not to say anything to others upon first bringing their retarded child home from the hospital). And so we said noth-

ing. We didn't tell the children either. . . . My older daughter was still in training (to become a nurse) so she wasn't there to tell, and finally around the end of October, around Christmas time, I just couldn't stand it any longer, and when we called our folks and our daughter, it was just before Christmas, she was with her grandparents. . . . I called and told them then. They took it very well. . . . And I called and told his (her husband's) sister, who I think is almost my best friend, a sister-in-law and one of the most nicest people around. But my husband still didn't want me to tell anybody else. In fact, he was quite angry when I told them.

Well, it broke him up. He tried not to show it, but I felt it because at that time he was shipping out. He was a merchant seaman. And Simon (her retarded child) was about six weeks old and he had to get a ship to leave, and I could see it all over him. He hated to leave us. And uh, he says he doesn't believe the doctor. You know that's when I, well, I sensed it, that he still doesn't. Where I could see, you know, that Simon is (retarded), but him, I guess it was this way and that way—not having any children you might as well say. And it broke him up I think quite a bit, because there was a difference in him to where we couldn't get along for a while together. I mean, I felt that was what was causing it. But then, after Simon was a couple of years old, there was a difference to where, well, it's something you've got to live with and things have changed. But I think now for instance, when he sees the granddaughters and Simon tries to keep up with them, you could see in his face, in fact Sunday he says—'if Simon was a normal child, he'd be eight years old; now look what he'd be doing.' So that's why I feel I guess, well, I have my four normal ones (from a former marriage), and he couldn't have one.

And my husband was very good (upon first hearing his child was retarded), although he was very, the fact is the night that we found out, I don't know, I called him or he called me, and I told him there was something wrong. And my husband is the type that really goes to pieces, and then I have to feel like I'm the strong one and have to kind of buck up and keep him from going to pieces. Fact is, seems to me, the doctor gave him a sedative that night. . . . Yeah, well of course my husband is very overprotective. And, uh, very overprotective with Joan, which is why his first reaction about sending her to school (the Pre-school) was rather on the negative side. He sees now that I was right about a lot of things, but he's still holding back on a lot of things. . . . I felt that he should have gone along with me more on trying to advance Joan. Because he can see now so much where it really has, the schooling and all, has meant so much to her. . . . What would she be like today (if he had kept her at home)? She's a bright child in her own way, but she needs someone to bring her out, and I don't think parents are the people to do it. Parents are not trained for that sort of thing.

Well, what can I say? How do you feel when you know that your child is, you know, . . . (the mother failed at this point to say the word herself) . . . This is a word that people used to shy away from. That was a kind of undercover thing, a well guarded secret. And I know it's more open and above board now, but I don't know, you certainly have some reservations or some feelings of anxiety. And I'm sure both of us (she and her husband) did. I think we could have helped Susan, had he not catered to her whims when she was small . . . my husband used to have a very bad habit when we first found out that she had a retardation problem. I have two other children. . . . He would say to them—now if Susan were doing something she wasn't supposed to be doing, and they knew that they weren't supposed to do it either, and they would tell her—don't do that, he would say—well now don't yell at her like that, you know Susan is not normal and . . . so we kind of got away from that. We had a little talk about that. . . . We used to try to make her say things (the child didn't start to talk until she was three), just anything, and she wouldn't. Because she used to suck her pacifier. And that was always in her mouth, and everybody was handing her things on a platter, you know, everything. So why take that out to talk? There was just no need to talk. And she wouldn't. She was really just about three years old before this happened. Then she started talking. She kept that pacifier until I guess she was about four years old. She was still walking around with it in her mouth. And I thought, oh, she would just have such awful tantrums when I would take it away from her. My husband would say . . . let her have it. Give it to her; let her go to bed and go to sleep, because I have to get up in the morning and go to work. A cousin of mine moved into the house with us for a very short period of time, . . . and everytime she saw it (the pacifier) she would put it in her overcoat pocket and take it with her. And she would say—now Susan you're too big for that. Keep it out of your mouth. And I'm gonna take it away. And Susan never cried when she spoke to her like that. She was very firm with her. And that is what stopped it. And every time my husband would go out and buy another one, this cousin would take it and hide it, and she wouldn't have it, so she stopped then. And you could see evidence of words coming out after that. She had nothing in the way, so she started to talk.

And sometimes it gets pretty frustrating. He feels like . . . you know, it made me feel like I was the hired hand, that whatever he (the husband) did was fine and whatever the child did was fine (their retarded child), but I couldn't chastise her. I said—now if you're gonna raise her, you do it; if she dirties her pants, you clean em. You be her mother and her father. You put her to bed; you comb her hair; and you take her to school. You do all these things. I said—now if I'm gonna play some role here, when I figure she's wrong, she's gonna get spanked. . . . But I think like I say, little by little, where it takes people about a year to adjust, it's taken us almost ten years. But I think we're finally gonna make it; we just might.

I have presented above some of the mothers' accounts of the ways in which the child's retardation affected the father and some of the consequences for the mother and child. With respect to the child, fathers were more overprotective and solicitous. Because the child was waited upon "hand and foot," it required little initiative or inventiveness on his part to get what he wanted and/or do as he pleased. This in turn tended to retard the child's development in two ways, firstly by encouraging a lack of initiative based upon necessity and secondly by assuming (as in the case of insanity) that the child is neither responsible nor accountable for his actions. The latter position resulted in excluding the child from a key feature of any normal socialization process, i.e., he was rarely subject to "limits" or to disciplinary action stemming from a breach of limits. In short the tendency was to view the child as either blameless (ultra-moral in a Rousseau sense in that he was incapable of being corrupted) or amoral, in that if he did wrong it was in no way by design.

Overprotection also led to the child's isolation. For example, fathers tended to feel that no one could or would care for the child as well as he and his wife and that the child should be kept from the "corrupting" influence of either outside helping agents or other retarded children, e.g. at the Pre-school. Add to this the father's initial desire to keep the child's retardation a secret and we can readily see some of the ways in which this isolation was extended.

The author wishes to emphasize at this point that the influence of the child's retardation upon the father and the consequences for the mother and child were not all negative. The net result of the child's retardation upon the parents varied from family to family. While nearly all families experienced a serious disruptive influence resulting from the child's retardation, this was for most parents associated with the initial shock of discovery and a period of adjustment. Granting that the adjustment period was sometimes a lengthy one (in a few cases, a satisfactory adjustment from the point of view of the parents' interaction has not yet been accomplished, even after five or six years), in most cases the parents succeeded in accommodating to their new situation, and in the final analysis found that having a retarded child had "all worked out for the best" or proved to be "a blessing in disguise."

Neal, you know, you talk about a child being very sensitive, he is. Whenever he sees my husband and I had an argument,

and I mean a serious one where we're screaming and hollering, and he (the husband) is trying to run in the closet for
his clothes (packing to leave), and I'm begging on my hands
and knees, Neal gets very upset. And he cries. He tries to
pull us apart. . . . I mean Neal sees that and he gets right
in there between us and he stands down there just crying his
heart out. And I mean he's enough to make you want to come
closer together. So I can actually say that if sometime we
didn't have Neal, we might not be together now. So we
can be very thankful to Neal for a lot of different things.
And especially with keeping us together too.

———————————

And, uh, you can't fool them (retarded children); you may
think that they don't know what's going on. I felt that way.
Now I learned you can't, uh, he knows (her retarded child)
what's going on. Even if my husband and I have a little
misunderstanding, he knows there is . . . he'll come in
between us and look at the both of us as if to say—well,
make up, forget it—you know. You can't fool them in any
way.

———————————

But as far as Stanley changing anything in our lives, if anything he's brought us closer together. And he's taught us a
love I'm sure we wouldn't learn from ten normal children. As
a matter of fact, my best description of Stanley is love. I
mean he is . . . sweetness personified. I can be in a rage
about something and turn around and see Stanley and his
smiling little face, and he'll really kind of calm me down . . .
Ken (her husband) is pretty easy-going and pretty level-
headed. Some days I don't like him too well, and I'm sure
he doesn't like me too well, but on the whole, we really have
a closeness to start with. But with Stanley, it has grown a
much closer feeling, and I think a deeper love between the
two of us. . . . And also it has taught us to be more and
more understanding of other people, a lot more tolerant of
things, you know. Well I thought I was tolerant before, but
I'm much more tolerant now. And cause sometimes you
listen to somebody else and you wish they'd shut up; they're
really bugging me. But since I've lived with Stanley and

been out here at the Pre-school, I can take much more time
at listening to somebody else's little problems. . . . Once
you've been through I think a real big emotional upset and a
real big hurt, you can understand all these other emotions in
yourself and other people. To me, I think Stanley has been
a wonderful experience.

. . . At the time I took her home (her retarded child) the
doctor had suggested leaving her in the hospital. I think
maybe he felt it might have been too much of a crisis for
me to handle or something. And of course I couldn't see that.
But I realize that if she'd been left in the hospital, she'd have
slept her life away. She'd have never lived through it. And
we'd have missed a beautiful experience.

However, a few parents who had not been able to satisfactorily
adapt to the situation felt that their child had exerted a disruptive, or in two cases, a disintegrative influence upon the family.

My mother came occasionally. She would come if we were
leaving. We went away for several weekends. I wouldn't say
we took this (the child's retardation) lying down. We didn't
just succumb and say—it's the end of our lives. And we'll
do everything for her, and no one else will ever touch her.
We didn't do that. And a lot of parents do. I know many
parents of handicapped children who didn't leave their children; I mean for a minute or the father is there. We did
struggle to stay together, to be a unit, you know, outside and
beyond her (the retarded child). We did retain and maintain
some kind of adult exchange, but it was a losing battle.

But even in these cases, the mothers expressed a warmth and
love for their retarded child and indicated that the interaction
between them (if not between the mother and father or mother
and other children) had grown closer and stronger with time.
In short, notwithstanding the family conflict the child was seen
to have generated, or the mother's feeling that "she had to live
with *it*," or the mother's homicidal feelings toward the child from
time to time, there developed between the mother and her re-

tarded child a state of strong ambivalence and frustration that somehow resolved itself in the child's favor. Even when infanticide was entertained, it was (from the parents' point of view) "for the child's own good." One mother expressed it this way:

> And I am sure that probably every parent that has talked to you has told you somewhat in the same manner that when you have more children, you know, the handicapped one is really the one you love the most. I don't know why it is, but it just exists; I don't know why. I had friends who had a deaf child, and this was the only one I had ever closely encountered with a handicapped child, and I could see they always felt sort of special toward her. And then, after I had Billy (her retarded child), I could see why. The idea because they're less than perfect, you know, that you don't care about them is not true.

Most mothers indicated, directly or indirectly from what they said, that their child's retardation had a strong influence upon their social life. Parents went out only rarely, and when they did, it was usually one at a time. One went while the other stayed at home with the child. If both parents and the retarded child went out at the same time, there were certain restrictions placed upon where they could go. It usually excluded them from public places and restricted social outings to taking car rides, a trip to the park, or socializing briefly with a few close friends or relatives. This pattern was perpetuated in part by choice and in part by necessity. In the first instance, it was true that parents often felt that no one could meet their child's needs quite as well as they could, since only they really understood them. However, with time and notwithstanding the father's tendency to be overprotective, both parents would have liked to go out and socialize the way they used to, i.e., as other parents with normal children do, and leave their child with a babysitter. Babysitting services or other forms of respite care for retarded children were practically non-existent. In most instances, the sitters were the child's grandparents or an older sib. This arrangement often proved a mixed blessing. Many parents stated that their retarded child had little influence upon their social life, because "we take him with us everywhere." This was generally true, since not taking the child often meant they could not leave. What was frequently understated was how infrequently they managed to socialize at all. This was especially true during the first few years. The following excerpts are illustrative of the constraining influence the child's retardation had upon the parents' social life:

> We try not to do anything that would involve having any body come in to sit. If my husband goes some place, like a ball game or something like that, he takes my son; that's their affair. Then other places where I can take all of them I will do that. Or, if I want to go out alone, I leave them (her children) with him (her husband). Or he does the same. Between the two of us, or we will do something where all of us can go out together. Other than that, we don't—our social life is really very limited, so we don't really get to do anything else that doesn't involve the children or where we can't have them actively participate with us. So I can't say that I do call on anybody. . . . Oh heavens, yes, sometimes I would dearly love to (get out and socialize more). I haven't really thought about that since I've been working the way I am now. But when I was working days, I don't know, my activities are much more now than they were when I was working days, of course, because this part of our life, this school here (the Pre-school) wasn't taken into account. We didn't have this to deal with. I was far less active, but I seem to be much more tired than I was, and when I would get home, that wasn't the place I wanted to go, because I knew my kids were there, and I wanted to go and relax, and you just can't, you know. But I don't have that feeling now. I'm much busier now than I was then (before entering the Pre-school). Maybe underneath there was that frustration of not knowing where to go next with Anne (her retarded child), or what to do . . . that probably had something to do with it. But all of that's settled in my mind now, and I just don't feel the tension that I felt before; I'm much more at ease with myself than I was then.

> You know, we really haven't had too much in the way of vacation trips. That's the only one we've taken (in six years).

And we did take him (her retarded child) along; it was a two-week trip. And other than that, we . . . now we've gone away for a weekend and left him with relatives. We've left him with my husband's parents or with an aunt and uncle of his. They have been very good to us and to John. His grandparents won't take John anymore. It's mainly because he's not trained (toilet-trained). Because they were very upset about my not training John. But I just never found a way to master it. . . . Yes, partly they (the grandparents) feel (that her failure to train him was some shortcoming on her part), and they took him when Joan (her second child) was born, and he was 3½. And they feel they had him trained. And you see when they brought him back, they said—he's all trained. All you have to do is put him on the potty after every meal. And, uh, it just didn't work out . . . it got to be . . . we had a very unpleasant experience centered around this whole business of toilet-training. . . . My husband stayed home for the first week after the baby. And he'd call them (the grandparents) and ask them how long did you . . . say you kept John on the potty? And then he'd say—well, he's been on 45 minutes; how much longer do you think we should keep him on? So we thought maybe this would get across to them that it just isn't working. . . . So finally after he got the infected rash which was all over his body (as a result of their toilet training effort) . . . we just decided that that was it. We weren't going to do it anymore. We were just going to let it go for a while. And once we did that, why then we could never get him back on the potty chair. He would never sit down on it. He just cried.

But now (of late as opposed to the first few years) I mean he (the retarded child) goes out with his daddy on Saturdays. On his day off, they're buddies, especially since he's been able to go to the bathroom. Frank (the husband) didn't take him a lot of places, not because he was ashamed of him that he couldn't go to the bathroom, but you don't take a child to a game and bring their pants and this and that along with them; he, you know, he made a mess because he was older.

... both of them (her mother and her sister) used to always be talking about how mean I am to Fred (her retarded son) and this and that. And I said—have you ever raised a boy? They said no. I said—well boys are different than girls, and you don't mollycoddle little boys and you don't sweet-talk little boys, cause they don't even hear you; they don't. And then my sister got involved working with groups in school, and she was working with little boys, and she found what little boys were like then. And she found out that you don't just say—now sweetheart, you don't do that; you might be able to say that to a little girl, but you don't talk like that to a little boy. ... My mother's fairly young; she's only in her early fifties. But my mother, uh, well she makes me very angry sometimes. ... You get so you're talking to her, and you no sooner get through than she has you repeating it three times. And by this time you're getting so mad, you say—mother, I just told you that. And then she gets mad at you because you're hollering at her. ... And then a lot of times she'll tell other people—oh she wishes she could help poor Evelyn (the mother) more with poor Fred, and you know, this and that, but ... she is not about to stay home and take time to take Fred to school or go pick him up or anything, you know. She's not about to get stuck with anything like that. So there are times when I just grit my teeth and I would like to say to her—mother, if you want to help, you could, but you don't.

She (the retarded child) gets into everything . . . everything . . . busy busy all the time. So that you always have her in your mind. You never have one minute that you can, you know, kind of blank out. So this four hours (spent daily at the Pre-school) is good for both her and for me.

We have seen how being confined a good deal to the home isolated not only the child but the parents. For the most part, the only persons that mothers could discuss their problems with were the grandparents, a close friend if they had one, and—on occasion—an older son or daughter. Unfortunately, attempted dialogue with the above persons often proved frustrating and/or unrewarding. Add to this the fact that many mothers felt (at least during the first few years) that they could not discuss their child's problems with their husbands, either because they were "quiet hard-working men who didn't talk much," or because the husband would not admit to the child's retardation, or because the husband spent so little time at home (compared with the time the mother spent in constant contact with the child) that there was little time to discuss the child's problems in any case, and one gets some notion of the extent of the frustration and isolation the mothers faced.

The mothers' discovery of the Pre-school changed all this in a very significant way. It ended their isolation as well as the child's and opened an avenue of meaningful discussion with others in similar circumstances who could understand and empathize with the mother's day to day problems. It also provided both mother and child with a respite from one another and afforded to each new and meaningful forms of interaction that neither had previously enjoyed. Not only were these forms of interaction new but they were in many instances the most meaningful either had managed to establish of late and at a point when the need was strongest.

Nothwithstanding the parents' desire to be able to socialize more, or have more free time, or witness the miraculous recovery of their child, had any or all of the above occurred they would have been viewed by many parents as mixed blessings. Some key reasons why parents felt this way are given in the following account:

> Doctor Jones asked me a question one day, and it goes like this: 'If you could have John turn normal right now, would you want it that way?' And I came out and I said—No. I said it so fast that I wanted to pull the words back in right after I said it, cause I feel like this, and some day I'm going to tell Dr. Jones this. I'm going to answer him in this way, and that is that I wouldn't want John to turn normal just like that, right now, because there are so many things that I enjoy out of John the way he is that I would miss actually, and besides that to just all of a sudden have so much time to yourself, it's kind of a shock to you too. I mean I'm going all the time after John; now if all of a sudden I've just got the time to sit and relax, that's going to bother me—just

drive me crazy. And so, now I should have really answered, that is I would have liked to see John turn to be normal, but to do it just gradually. Even if it takes five years.

Had the child miraculously recovered or the diagnosis proved false or the child died or been institutionalized, it would have meant for the parents, and especially the mothers, two things. On the one hand, they would have had more free time (which was something mothers both wanted and were no longer accustomed to), and they and their husbands could have, in time, taken up a more active social life. On the other hand, it would have destroyed in one fell swoop a way of life that the parents had established since the birth of their child, i.e. for the last four to eight years.

> *He (the retarded child) was the one* child who was not expected to grow up; who was disciplined, praised, teased, humored, coddled, was expected to have no will of his own, but *around whom family members, especially the parents, rotated.*[24] (Emphasis added.)

As a result, while the child's significant improvement or complete recovery was something all parents hoped for, they did not do so without some feelings of ambivalence. The above was especially true for the mothers, only two of whom were employed outside of the home. The fathers' days were occupied at work. For the mothers, the allocation and distribution of time revolved almost exclusively around their retarded child. Even when there were other children in the family, they were usually at school or, in the case of older children, married, in the army, or away at college.

The above discussion has outlined for the reader some of the reasons why and the ways in which parents of retarded children had managed to redefine the effects of their child's retardation so as to convince themselves that it was, in fact, "a blessing in disguise."

Effects upon the Sibs

Eleven of the fourteen cases in the author's series involved the presence of one or more sibs. We have already discussed the retarded child's effects upon the parents. What were his effects upon the sibs? The author's findings tend to support those of Kramm that ". . . most of the normal brothers and sisters were sympathetic and helpful. Only a few were not."[25] Mothers reported that sibs loved the retarded child, got along very well with him, and were understanding and helpful.

Notwithstanding the mothers' tendency to preface their accounts of interactions between their retarded child and other children with this cheerful and optimistic note, it soon became clear that things were in many respects something less than ideal. The following excerpts are illustrative of the general tone:

> Joan (her retarded child) is nowhere near as much a handicap as some children, but still it's kind of a growing experience. For a family, it's a real testing experience; it was hard on the others, on the children who were younger. Not younger than her, but we have two teenage boys . . . I think Len (one of the two boys) took it harder than anybody at first . . . Len is . . . well, there are two boys at home. Len is 15 and John is 13. And Len was, I'm sure that Len was particularly affected because of the fact that he couldn't say anything to her (the retarded daughter), but he called John a retard. Every time he got mad at him, John was a retard see. Well this, if you understand anything at all about this, you realize what it was. You know, it's his way of reacting. And John in turn, John of course being the youngest of six boys, was in a particularly bad spot, because everybody picked on him you know. He had to battle before he could stand up . . . and he has had problems . . . John does tease Joan in his own way; see he's got subtle ways, and of course she has learned, like all children learn, that if she screeches when somebody looks crosseyed at her they'll get into trouble. . . . So it's meant problems in the family.

> Fine. Fine. (how the sibs relate to retarded child) The older one gets annoyed with me, mostly because she thinks I'm spoiling her, but she's an R.N. so she thinks she knows all the answers. And she's very good with her; if she had more time. . . . I think she could discipline her better than I can.

The 19-year-old is in the army, but he's sending a small amount every month to put in the bank for her. And he was real good when he came home on leave, took her for walks and watched her for me and played with her. The 16-year-old she likes best of all. And he can take her or leave her. When he plays with her, she knows he really wants to play with her. He's taking time out to play, and when he doesn't want to be bothered, he just doesn't want to be bothered and she knows it, but she seems to like him best of all. Anne (a younger daughter) plays with her and then after a while Anne gets tired because she can't keep up with her, and she gets lonesome for other playmates. We don't have, as I said, we don't have any children in our neighborhood. . . . There has never been any sign of animosity at all. They've done marvelously well. . . . Once in a while, little Anne feels she'd like to have a little more attention, and she really doesn't get enough. I'd like to give her more, but she's a very happy child, and I can't see that there's any lasting effect. . . . I think she should have a little more attention than she does get. But the others you see (the older sibs), one is already gone, and the other keeps threatening to leave cause the family is so noisy and all.

The one that Evan (the retarded child) has hurt the most has been Ruth (her 5-year-old daughter) because Ruth being a baby, whenever something happened to Evan, she was pushed aside. Where I can actually say that it grows on the youngster's mind, why is he getting it when he's older and I'm still a baby and I'm not getting it? Things just don't go that way, now do they? And I feel that she will always have that in the back of her mind, because even now she gets a little resentful at times when Evan does something that he's got to have my attention for quicker than hers. And it's just like with potty training. Ruth feels, well he's older; why isn't he? (potty trained) Why do I have to be when he's still older than I am? Why am I getting pushed above Evan? Why do I have to do everything before he does when it comes to learning things? But then on the other hand, why does he come before I do? So I mean it's quite confusing to her and I feel that Ruth feels it more than anyone else. If I could start all over again, I really don't know what changes I could make, but I could only hope that Ruth could come before Evan. Because I feel that she . . . would have come along a lot faster. I mean Ruth still has some accidents at night; she gets up the next morning, and it doesn't bother her at all because she comes out and what am I doing but taking diapers off of Evan. Why should it bother her? I mean she's still the baby and feels why can't I wet the bed. And I mean it was the same way with walking; she was slow at walking, very hard to take the bottle away from and everything else because Evan still had all these things and she was getting away from it. . . .

She (her seven-year-old daughter) gets along good with Evan. . . . She slaps him down whenever he needs it. But she won't let him get by with nothing. Well, just like I've told her with this here pushing habit that Evan gets into, I said whenever Evan pushes you, turn around and push him right back, just make sure he doesn't get hurt. I says don't push him into the wall or onto the bookcase or bang his head into a cabinet or something. I says just push him. Let him sit down in the middle of the floor but let him know that you don't approve of it.

And it is a little hard for his (the retarded child's) sister, because, you know, he destroys her things—eating her crayons and tearing up her books, carting off her doll furniture and breaking it, . . . he doesn't deliberately break it, but he treats it so rough that it breaks. You know, he bounces it along, scratches up the walls. . . .

Yeah, fine (how the sibs get along with retarded child). In fact, they tend to overprotect him. And of course like I say they still get stuck with the duty of taking him out. I can't trust him out by himself, so it's kind of six of one half dozen of the other, but on the whole they're very very good to him. And even our 13-year-old, we've been having a great deal of problems right now; he's the one that's closest to Peter (the retarded child), and he's very good with him. And it's funny. When I first told the three of them (that their brother was retarded), they reacted very differently. The oldest boy cried, ran into his room and cried. My daughter took Peter into her room and she was reading a book to him, trying to teach him the alphabet—A,B,C. And then the third one, I just kind of felt the whole thing kind of went over his head, I'm not sure how much he got out of it. So every once in a while, I have to remind him that Peter is a little slower and we need to treat him a little differently. But he's the one that's got . . . he was the baby until Peter came along, so I think there's a little jealousy there.

But . . . it seemed like the day that I was coming home from the hospital, my son-in-law was bringing us home from the hospital, and I also wondered what my children would think (of the retarded child). And . . . it took me a week (to tell them), and here they said there was nothing wrong with him. And here it's hard! And I just feel for the ones whose children never show a difference (no visual signs of retardation) and it's harder even for them (the parents and sibs to accept the retardation).

It was generally true that sibs were understanding and helpful toward the retarded child. However, younger sibs seemed to have felt more of a disruptive influence. They were jealous of the greater amount of time and attention shown by parents to the retarded child and his exemption from the demands and expectations associated with normal children. Younger children tended to view this differential treatment as parental favoritism, especially when the normal child was so young that he could not grasp what the retardation meant and/or if he was the only other child in the family. In general then, the older the sibs, the more helpful and accepting they were.

With sibs, as with adults (and outside helping agents), the general attitude towards the retarded child was paternal. The notion that the retarded child would remain "retarded" and "a child" into adulthood was a key determinant of the sib-retarded child interaction. In the author's series, the age range of the retarded children was from 4 to 8. Even at this young age, a younger sib would refer to an older retarded brother or sister as "the kid." This outlook perpetuated itself into adulthood.

> Although in life age a few of the mongoloid young people in this study were adults, they were regarded as children. One sister of a 32-year-old mongoloid brother coaxed, 'come, honey, eat your dinner like a good boy.' The younger brother of a 16-year-old mongoloid sister inquired, 'have you been a good girl today?'. Still other children referred to their mongoloid brother or sister as 'Little Jack' or 'Little Jane,' irrespective of age. If the retarded child was the first born, his brothers and sisters grew up past him and looked back on him as the last born and as the 'baby' of the family.[26]

In short, the nature of the retarded child-sib relationship from childhood to adulthood was, depending upon age differences and family size, essentially one of "play" and/or jealousy and rivalry. Much less emphasis was placed upon the role of the sib as teacher. This is unfortunate, since sibs often spent, in the aggregate, a considerable amount of time with the retarded child. If both parents and sibs adopted the perspective that the retarded child was both responsible and accountable for his actions (as indeed most are), i.e. if they treated him seriously, these forms of interaction might have progressed from "play" to more advanced educational and social forms of exchange. The beneficial effects of home educational and training programs upon the child's future level of competence has been noted elsewhere.[27] That retarded children are denied the benefit of such programs and/or access to some outside educational programs, needlessly results for many in their ultimate institutionalization.

FOOTNOTES—CHAPTER III

1. See for example:
   Elizabeth R. Kramm, *The Families of Mongoloid Children*, Washington, D.C.: Children's Bureau, U.S. Department of Health, Education and Welfare, 1963, p. 6.
   S. Olshonsky, "Chronic Sorrow: a response to having a mentally defective child," *Children*, 1962, 43, pp. 191-194.

E. Smith, "Emotional factors as revealed in the intake process with parents of defective children," *American Journal of Mental Deficiency*, 1952, 56, pp. 806-811.

2. Roy De Verl Willey and Kathleen Barnette Waite, *The Mentally Retarded Child*, Springfield, Illinois: Charles C Thomas, 1964, p. 197.

3. *San Francisco Chronicle*, September 26, 1968, p. 7. For an interesting parallel, see a previous essay by the author entitled "The Use of Religion in Constructing the Moral Justification of Suicide," in *Deviance and Respectability: The Social Construction of Moral Meanings*, edited by Jack D. Douglas (In press, Basic Books).

4. D. J. West, *Murder Followed by Suicide*, Cambridge, Massachusetts: Harvard University Press, 1966, p. 48.

5. *Ibid.*, pp. 49 and 82.

6. *Ibid.*, p. 48.

7. *PCMR Message*, April 1968, p. 3.

8. *San Francisco Chronicle*, October 13, 1968, p. 21.

9. *The Edge of Change: A Report to the President on Mental Retardation Program Trends and Innovations, with Recommendations on Residential Care, Manpower and Deprivation*, President's Committee on Mental Retardation, Washington, D.C., Government Printing Office, 1968, pp. 12, 16.

10. Robert B. Edgerton, *The Cloak of Competence: Stigma in the Lives of the Retarded*, Berkeley: University of California Press, 1967, pp. 59, 71.

11. *Ibid.*, pp. 76-77.

12. *Ibid.*, p. 146.

13. *Ibid.*, p. 147.

14. *The Wall Street Journal*, November 6, 1968, p. 1.

15. *Ibid.*, pp. 1 and 21.

16. Erving Goffman, *Asylums*, Garden City, New York: Doubleday & Co., 1961, pp. 1-124.

17. Edgerton, *op. cit.*, p. 10.

18. Kramm, *op. cit.*, p. 35.

19. *Ibid.*, p. 43.

20. *Ibid.*, p. 28.

21. *Ibid.*, p. 33, 31, and 34 respectively.

22. See for example:
Alice V. Anderson, "Orienting Parents to a Clinic for the Retarded," *Children*, 1962, 9, pp. 178-182.
A. Hersh, "Case Work with Parents of Retarded Children," *Social Work*, 1961, 6, pp. 61-66.

23. See for example:
Fanny Stang, "Parents' Guidance and the Mentally Retarded Child," *Public Health* (London), 1957, 71, pp. 220, 234-236.
Mary L. Yates and Ruth Lederer, "Small, Short-Term Group Meetings with Parents of Children with Mongolism," *American Journal of Mental Deficiency*, 1961, 65, pp. 467-472.
M. J. Begab, *The Mentally Retarded Child: A Guide to Services of Social Agencies*, Washington, D.C.: U.S. Government Printing Office, 1963.

34

J. W. Oberman, "The Physician and Parents of the Retarded Child," *Children*, 1963, 10, pp. 109-113.
24. Kramm, *op. cit.*, p. 18.
25. *Ibid.*, p. 18.
26. *Ibid.*, pp. 20-21.
27. See for example:
Nigel Hunt's *The World of Nigel Hunt: The Diary of a Mongoloid Youth*, New York: Garrett Publications, 1967. It notes how a mother of a retarded child, having been told by ". . . the senior officer concerned with mental affairs . . . 'oh, yes, a little mongoloid. Quite ineducable. Do you want him put away?',", proceeded to educate him. The child in question grew up to author the book.
Ray R. Battin and Olaf C. Haugh, *Speech and Language Delay: A Home Training Program*. Springfield, Illinois, Charles C Thomas, 1964.
W. M. Cruickshank, *The Brain-Injured Child in Home, School, and Community*, Syracuse, New York: Syracuse University Press, 1967.
Ruth Mallison, *Education as Therapy*, Seattle Washington: Special Child Publications, 1968.
Edward L. French and Clifford J. Scott, *How You Can Help your Retarded Child*, Philadelphia, Pennsylvania: J. B. Lippincott Co., 1967.

CHAPTER IV
Summary and Conclusions

The author has attempted to delineate the past, present and projected careers of a group of 14 retarded children, and the forms of medical, educational and familial interactions these careers occasioned, as well as to outline the consequences of these interactions for the child, his parents and his sibs. It has been noted that retarded children have frequent and sometimes extended contact with physicians for treatment and/or evaluational reasons, especially in early childhood. The nature of these interactions was viewed by most parents as unsatisfactory. Their outcomes for the parents and their children ranged from disruptive to disastrous. The author suggests that greater emphasis ought to be placed upon educating and sensitizing physicians to the management of information transfer in routine and crisis situations involving retarded children and their parents. Furthermore, it is the author's opinion that medical personnel would do well to reevaluate their current outlooks on mental retardation and acquaint themselves more with the ambiguous and contradictory nature of the current medical model and its consequences for the physician, the retarded child and his family. More effort and money needs to be redirected from medical settings to educational, rehabilitational and social science research efforts. The current priority funding structure, allocating the lion's share of all available mental retardation funds to medical settings, is inequitable, in that it tends to benefit only a very small percentage of all the retarded.

Educational programs for the retarded and teacher curriculums and systems of credentialing badly need looking into. According to the teachers' own accounts, their special training had little if any relevance to teaching the retarded. The reorganization and expansion of educational programs for the retarded, and a greater voice by teachers in curriculum planning, are sorely needed. Because of current organizational arrangements, teachers feel themselves alienated from a meaningful dialogue with administrators and believe that those who are least in touch with the problems of educating the retarded are most strategically situated to dictate the methods and goals of "special education". Under the circumstances, it is not surprising to find that administrators have thus far had little success in realizing the programs they envisioned. The "operational definition" of educating the retarded currently held by teachers of the retarded involved two key features, i.e. "playing it by ear" and "it's good if it works." In short, there is in practice no program of education for the retarded, let alone a compulsory program of mass education that six million retarded children and adults require.

In the last chapter, I have discussed some of the effects of the child's retardation upon the family. This aspect was dealt with in two sections, i.e. the effects upon the parents and the effects upon the sibs. Fathers more than mothers seemed to have been adversely affected. They tended to be "overprotective," secretive and less able to accept the diagnosis of mental retardation. This resulted at the outset (but less so as time went on) in disruptive influences within the family. The father's tendency to overprotect the child from "corrupting outside influences" worked to isolate the entire family, but especially the mother and retarded child. The mothers' acquaintance with the Pre-school did much to counteract this isolation for both her and the child. In spite of the child's disruptive influence upon the family, he also exerted a binding effect that the parents (especially the mothers) tended to see in the overview as "all for the best." In time, most parents were able to redefine the effect of the child's retardation upon the family, so that in the final analysis it was seen as a "blessing in disguise."

Finally, the nature of the interactions between the sibs and the retarded child was considered. Sibs (especially older sibs) were generally helpful and understanding and played well with the retarded child. Because sibs tended to see the retarded child (as adults do) as incapable of "growing up," the nature of their interactions with them never progressed, as with normal children, from a play form to more elaborate and advanced educational and social forms of interaction. That the retarded remain "children" is seen by the author to stem to a large extent from the prior background expectancies of the persons the child encounters in the course of his career who, convinced he is incapable of growing up, treat him as though this were not a problematic assumption. The result is a self-fulfilling prophecy. Many retarded children who have had the benefit of home and outside educational programs where this was not explicitly or implicitly assumed have shown marked improvement. It was also noted that younger sibs were less able than older sibs to adjust to the retarded child, with the result that their interactions were more often characterized by rivalry and jealousy.

If there is a leit motif to the author's work, it is that lay persons and professionals alike should hold in abeyance the routine acceptance of most general assumptions currently held about mental retardation until such time as there are better grounds for accepting them. "Adequately diagnosed" retardation is irreversible, "trainable" children are incapable of learning to read with comprehension, retarded children "don't grow up," (e.g. they die early or can't develop intellectually beyond the age of 12), I.Q. is an accurate or at least fair assessment of the child's current and future intellectual potential, etc.—these are only a few of the assumptions routinely made by lay persons and/or professionals.

It is true that not all professionals believe all of the above. However, these and other "facts" were presented by doctors, psychologists, social workers and others to the parents in the author's study. The author has dealt throughout the book with these routinely made assumptions and their consequences for the retarded child and his family.

On the basis of my work and that of others, I can only conclude that a good rule of thumb would be to assume at the outset that the number of unknowns in the area of mental retardation is sufficient to preclude a definitive diagnosis and prognosis for any given child and to proceed "as if" the child may after all recover or "anything can happen," and treat the future of any given retarded person as problematic. Both the author and others in the field have presented well-documented material in the form of individual cases and/or group data indicating that "anything" has already happened with respect to the expectations and predictions of many lay and professional persons.[1] A vivid illustration of this was the author's recent encounter with a social worker whose husband is a doctor at a local hospital. She told of how he was amazed one day to find himself in the emergency room treating a retarded adolescent for a suicide attempt in the form of an overdose of sleeping pills. A suicide attempt after all requires an act of volition and the doctor had not until that moment believed a retarded person capable of such an act.

If this study of the careers of mentally retarded children has served to reorient the reader to reevaluate and/or hold the above and other "well-known facts" about mental retardation in abeyance, and proceed instead to attempt to understand and assist the retarded from a more neutral and (because of the nature of current assumptions) optimistic stand, the author may have succeeded in helping to prove wrong his earlier pessimistic appraisal of the prospects of initiating comprehensive educational, rehabilitational and medical programs for the retarded. Whether or not these programs will be realized in the foreseeable future remains questionable. It is often said that only change is certain. Let us hope that things change for the better.

FOOTNOTE—CHAPTER IV

1. For example, see:
   Nigel Hunt (Chapter III above, footnote 27).
   A study of I.Q. in Onondaga County, New York.
   A study by Rosenberg and Jacobson, ". . . in which randomly selected children showed an average gain over controls of 25 I.Q. points in one year after teachers were told, falsely, that remarkable I.Q. gains could be expected from these children," in *Teachers and Testing*, by David A. Goslin, New York: Russell Sage Foundation, 1967, discussed in a book review by Patricia Kayo Sexton in the *American Sociological Review*, August 1968, Vol. 33, No. 4, p. 662.
   The reference to "trainable" children reading with comprehension noted on p. 131.
   The author's work, "The Social Organization of Mental Retardation Categories," in *Deviancy in American Society*, edited by Jack D. Douglas, Basic Books, in press.